LiveCode Mobile Development Beginner's Guide

Create fun-filled, rich apps for Android and iOS with LiveCode

Colin Holgate

BIRMINGHAM - MUMBAI

LiveCode Mobile Development Beginner's Guide

First published: July 2012

Production Reference: 1190712

Published by Packt Publishing Ltd.
Livery Place
35 Livery Street
Birmingham B3 2PB, UK.

ISBN 978-1-84969-248-9

www.packtpub.com

Cover Image by Artie Ng (artherng@yahoo.com.au)

Credits

Author

Colin Holgate

Reviewers

Björnke von Gierke

Andreas Rozek

Acquisition Editor

Mary Jasmine Nadar

Lead Technical Editor

Susmita Panda

Technical Editors

Rati Pillai

Lubna Shaikh

Project Coordinator

Leena Purkait

Proofreader

Stephen Silk

Indexers

Hemangini Bari

Tejal Daruwale

Production Coordinator

Arvindkumar Gupta

Cover Work

Arvindkumar Gupta

About the Author

Colin Holgate was originally trained as a telecommunications technician in the Royal Air Force, but with the advent of the personal computer era he transitioned to work as a technical support engineer for companies that included Apple Computer UK.

In 1992 he moved to the USA to become a full time multimedia programmer, working for The Voyager Company. In that role he programmed several award winning CD-ROMs, including *A Hard Day's Night* and *This Is Spinal Tap*.

For the last 12 years Colin has worked for Funny Garbage, a New York City based interactive media design company. In addition to using Adobe Director and Adobe Flash for online and kiosk applications, he has used LiveCode to create in-house and client production tools. At the *RunRevLive Conference* in 2011, Colin entered and won a contest to create a mobile application made with LiveCode.

About the Reviewers

Björnke von Gierke started scripting with HyperCard when he was a teenager. He began to use LiveCode as a hobby and because he wanted to create a computer game, for which he never did any coding. Soon his focus changed to several community initiatives and free add-ons for LiveCode developers, as well as small database applications for local non-profit organizations. By now he has worked and, more importantly, played with LiveCode for more than 10 years.

Andreas Rozek is a physicist (albeit with many years of experience in EU research projects in the area of multimedia and mobile telecommunications). But, as his hope (namely that "Computers should be fun and support people rather than bother or even impede them") still needs to become common reality, he essentially searches - day in, day out - for development environments well suited "for the rest of us" and tries to construct "humane solutions" by means of intelligently coupled systems, intuitive operating concepts, attractive user interfaces and fault-tolerant procedures.

LiveCode is both, a programming language which can easily be used by "casual programmers", and a development environment which helps in constructing visually appealing user interfaces for a wide variety of target devices. For that reason, Andreas is glad to have gotten the opportunity to review this wonderful book which should help you in converting your ideas into actual mobile applications.

www.PacktPub.com

Support files, eBooks, discount offers and more

You might want to visit www.PacktPub.com for support files and downloads related to your book.

Did you know that Packt offers eBook versions of every book published, with PDF and ePub files available? You can upgrade to the eBook version at www.PacktPub.com and as a print book customer, you are entitled to a discount on the eBook copy. Get in touch with us at service@packtpub.com for more details.

At www.PacktPub.com, you can also read a collection of free technical articles, sign up for a range of free newsletters and receive exclusive discounts and offers on Packt books and eBooks.

http://PacktLib.PacktPub.com

Do you need instant solutions to your IT questions? PacktLib is Packt's online digital book library. Here, you can access, read and search across Packt's entire library of books.

Why Subscribe?

* Fully searchable across every book published by Packt
* Copy and paste, print and bookmark content
* On demand and accessible via web browser

Free Access for Packt account holders

If you have an account with Packt at www.PacktPub.com, you can use this to access PacktLib today and view nine entirely free books. Simply use your login credentials for immediate access.

Table of Contents

Preface

Everyone you know has a smart mobile device of some kind. You probably own several! The general idea of having utility applications on a phone is not new, and even cell phone and PDA games have existed for years, but the way that the iPhone used touch instead of a stylus or keyboard, and gestures to reduce the number of steps to do something, was a game changer.

The iPhone was released in June 2007, and Android OS in September 2008. If you wanted to create something that worked on both platforms you had to learn two development environments and languages; Objective-C for iPhone, and Java for Android.

In the desktop world there are several development tools that do allow you to publish to both Mac and Windows, as well as Linux in the case of LiveCode. The most successful of these tools are Adobe Director, Adobe Flash, Unity, and LiveCode. Publishing to iOS is being worked on for Director, which will mean that all four tools are also suitable for developing for mobile.

Those tools have different strengths. In some cases the strengths relate to the nature of the applications you can make, and in other cases it relates to how accessible the tool is to people who are not hardcore programmers. If you want to make a high quality 3D game, Unity would be the best choice, with Director and then Flash as other choices. If you need a lot of character animations, then Flash would be the best choice, with Director being a good alternate.

If the important thing is how approachable the tool is, then LiveCode wins easily. It's also just as valid a choice for making the majority of apps you might wish to. In fact, for apps that are a set of single screens, as would be the case for most utility apps, as well as for board and puzzle games, LiveCode is better suited than the other tools. It also has better access to native interface elements; with the other tools you usually have to create graphics that resemble the look of native iOS and Android controls, instead of accessing the real thing.

With its easy to use English-like programming language, and the "stack of cards" metaphor, LiveCode lets you concentrate more on creating the app you want to make, and less on the technicalities of the development environment.

What this book covers

Chapter 1, LiveCode Fundamentals, will introduce you to the LiveCode environment, and to its English-like programming language. Experienced LiveCode users can skip this chapter, but for someone new to LiveCode this chapter will take you through creating a simple calculator app as a way to make you familiar with the various tools and hierarchy of LiveCode.

Chapter 2, Getting Started with LiveCode Mobile, describes in detail how to set up your Mac or Windows computer so that you are ready to develop and publish mobile apps. This chapter will take you all the way from signing up as an iOS and Android developer, to creating and testing your first LiveCode mobile app.

Chapter 3, Building User Interfaces, shows how to use some of the standard mobile features, such as date pickers, photo album, and camera. This chapter will also show how to make your own buttons with an iOS look to them, and how to use the LiveCode add-on, MobGUI, to make your life easier!

Chapter 4, Using Remote Data and Media, discusses the structure of your apps, where to place your code, and how to read from and write to external text files. You will also create a mobile app that is a "web-scraper", capable of extracting links and media from a web page, and to show or play media from that page.

Chapter 5, Making a Jigsaw Puzzle Application, will show you how to process image data, and to use the information to create a color picker, detect regions, and to make a collision map. You will then create a full jigsaw puzzle application that takes its image from the photo album or device camera.

Chapter 6, Making a Reminders Application, examines what information is needed to represent a "reminder", and how to set up notification events so that you are alerted at a specified date and time. You will make a reminders app that can create a list of such events, and even list those events based on your current location.

Chapter 7, Deploying to Your Device, is a reference chapter that describes all of the mobile publishing settings. The chapter also shows how to send apps to beta testers, and how to get started with submitting your finished app to the various app stores.

Appendix A, Extending LiveCode, describes add-ons to LiveCode that will make your mobile apps look better, or that extend the mobile capabilities of LiveCode.

What you need for this book

In addition to LiveCode itself, you would need a Mac or PC, iOS and/or Android devices, and an amount of money if you follow the parts about signing up as a mobile developer! For iOS development you will need access to an Intel based Mac for some of the steps. The example code requires LiveCode version 5.5 or later.

Who this book is for

The ideal reader for this book would be someone who already knows LiveCode, is interested in creating mobile apps, and wants to save the many hours it would take to track down all of the information on how to get started! *Chapter 1, LiveCode Fundamentals*, will help readers who know programming but are not familiar with LiveCode enough for them to benefit from the remainder of the book.

Conventions

In this book, you will find several headings appearing frequently.

To give clear instructions of how to complete a procedure or task, we use:

Time for action – heading

1. Action 1

2. Action 2

3. Action 3

Instructions often need some extra explanation so that they make sense, so they are followed with:

What just happened?

This heading explains the working of tasks or instructions that you have just completed.

You will also find some other learning aids in the book, including:

Pop quiz – heading

These are short multiple choice questions intended to help you test your understanding.

Have a go hero – heading

These set practical challenges and give you ideas for experimenting with what you have learned.

You will also find a number of styles of text that distinguish different kinds of information. Here are some examples of these styles, and an explanation of their meaning.

Code words in text are shown as follows: "In the empty line between `on mouseUp` and `end mouseUp`, **type** `numberPressed the label of me`."

A block of code is set as follows:

```
on clearPressed
    put true into newNumber
    put 0 into field "display"
    put 0 into currentTotal
    put 0 into currentValue
    put empty into currentCommand
end clearPressed
```

Any command-line input or output is written as follows:

```
export PATH=$PATH:/Users/yourusername/Documents/android-sdk-macosx/
platform-tools
```

New terms and **important words** are shown in bold. Words that you see on the screen, in menus or dialog boxes for example, appear in the text like this: "Take note of the items on the right-hand side, **User Samples**, **Tutorials**, **Resources**, and **Dictionary**.".

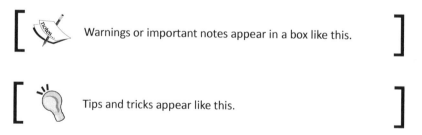

Warnings or important notes appear in a box like this.

Tips and tricks appear like this.

Reader feedback

Feedback from our readers is always welcome. Let us know what you think about this book—what you liked or may have disliked. Reader feedback is important for us to develop titles that you really get the most out of.

To send us general feedback, simply send an e-mail to feedback@packtpub.com, and mention the book title through the subject of your message.

If there is a topic that you have expertise in and you are interested in either writing or contributing to a book, see our author guide at www.packtpub.com/authors.

Customer support

Now that you are the proud owner of a Packt book, we have a number of things to help you to get the most from your purchase.

Downloading the example code

You can download the example code files for all Packt books you have purchased from your account at http://www.packtpub.com. If you purchased this book elsewhere, you can visit http://www.packtpub.com/support and register to have the files e-mailed directly to you.

Errata

Although we have taken every care to ensure the accuracy of our content, mistakes do happen. If you find a mistake in one of our books—maybe a mistake in the text or the code—we would be grateful if you would report this to us. By doing so, you can save other readers from frustration and help us improve subsequent versions of this book. If you find any errata, please report them by visiting http://www.packtpub.com/support, selecting your book, clicking on the **errata submission form** link, and entering the details of your errata. Once your errata are verified, your submission will be accepted and the errata will be uploaded to our website, or added to any list of existing errata, under the Errata section of that title.

Piracy

Piracy of copyright material on the Internet is an ongoing problem across all media. At Packt, we take the protection of our copyright and licenses very seriously. If you come across any illegal copies of our works, in any form, on the Internet, please provide us with the location address or website name immediately so that we can pursue a remedy.

Please contact us at `copyright@packtpub.com` with a link to the suspected pirated material.

We appreciate your help in protecting our authors, and our ability to bring you valuable content.

Questions

You can contact us at `questions@packtpub.com` if you are having a problem with any aspect of the book, and we will do our best to address it.

1
LiveCode Fundamentals

Is this chapter for you?

LiveCode has an English-like programming language, a graphical development environment, and an easy-to-understand structural metaphor. When you create an application, you spend more time thinking about how to implement the different features, and less about the complexities of the tool you are using. But if you've never used LiveCode before, it's still going to be unfamiliar at first. This chapter will bring you up to speed, ready for the later chapters that will require that you are more familiar with the terminology and features of the tool.

LiveCode is easy, but there are thousands of easy things to learn! Throughout the book we will look at the latest of those easy things, particularly those related to mobile applications, but first we should go over some of the basics.

In this chapter we shall:

- Become familiar with the LiveCode environment
- Investigate the hierarchy of a LiveCode "stack"
- Create a simple calculator application
- Learn about the many different interface controls

So let's get on with it...

Background history and metaphors

Many development tools just present a programming language and interfaces to system routines. Higher-level tools often present the same things, but structured in such a way that you can think of real world metaphors for the different aspects of the tool. LiveCode is very much like that, and its metaphor is a **stack of cards**. This metaphor originated with Apple Computer's HyperCard authoring tool, created by Bill Atkinson in the mid-1980s. The first version of HyperCard was released in August 1987, and it became a huge hit in both education and multimedia. Companies such as The Voyager Company published entire product lines that were created using HyperCard.

Other companies produced tools that were very much like HyperCard, but that also tried to give the user more features than were in HyperCard. The most prominent of those tools were SuperCard, Plus, and MetaCard. Plus went on to have an interesting life, the product itself became Windows-only (it was cross-platform at first), but later the same code ended up in the cross-platform tool Oracle Media Objects. All of these tools perpetuated the metaphor of a stack of cards.

MetaCard was most notable for the fact that it was multi-platform, not just cross-platform. **Stacks**, the general term used for documents created by these tools, made with MetaCard could run on Unix and Linux systems, as well as Mac and Windows. Alas, it was somewhat ugly! The Scottish company RunRev made a product that was an attempt to present MetaCard in a more appealing way. Eventually RunRev acquired MetaCard, and since 2003 RunRev has continued to build upon MetaCard, using the product name "Runtime Revolution", later renamed to LiveCode.

Under the HyperCard variation of the metaphor, documents consisted of cards that held buttons, fields, and bitmap graphics, backgrounds that held a set of cards, and stacks that held a set of backgrounds. LiveCode takes a slightly different approach, and rather than having backgrounds that hold cards, it allows you to group any set of interface controls and set those to act as if they are a background entity. This ends up being more flexible, though slightly alien to people who have used HyperCard a lot.

Both HyperCard and LiveCode provide ways to extend the hierarchy further. You will be able to take other stacks and put them into use. To save rewriting the same set of functions in every stack, you might choose to have a stack dedicated to those functions, and then add that stack to the "stackinsuse", using the command:

```
start using stack "utility stack"
```

Additionally you can write **externals**, which are commands and functions written in the C language, which can extend LiveCode's abilities even further.

You do have LiveCode, don't you?

If you haven't yet installed LiveCode, go to this web page: `http://www.runrev.com/downloads/`. You will need to create an account to be able to download the trial version. If you plan to go on to buy LiveCode, read through this page: `http://www.runrev.com/products/livecode/license-types-overview/` to understand the many license variations there are. As a rough guide, based on the price at the time of writing, to create mobile applications that are free, it would be $99, or if you wanted to make apps that you could charge for, it would be $499. Each extra platform that you want to publish to would be another $99.

Once you have downloaded the trial version, or bought one of the licenses, why not go ahead and launch it!

Learning the lay of the land

When you first open LiveCode you are shown a Start Center window, which functions as a way to open recent documents, a list of links to forums, and getting started information. It also provides a way to view promotional information. It does no harm to keep that window open, but if you do happen to close it you can reopen the Start Center from the **Help** menu.

As you look at LiveCode for the first time you will notice a toolbar along the top of the screen, just below the menu bar. Take note of the items on the right-hand side, **User Samples**, **Tutorials**, **Resources**, and **Dictionary**. These areas are filled with information that will help you to get started with LiveCode. The **Dictionary** is something that you will use a lot, and just browsing through the entries will either answer your immediate question or give you advanced information about issues you'll run into later.

The **Help** menu also provides access to a **User Guide** and several release note files. Consult the **User Guide** to read in more depth about features mentioned here.

Online lessons

In addition to the resources you see inside LiveCode itself, there is a tremendous amount of information and tutorials on the RunRev website. A good starting point would be: `http://lessons.runrev.com/`

The following screenshot shows the windows and palettes that we're going to be using for now, as well as the document window, which shows a simple calculator that we will soon build:

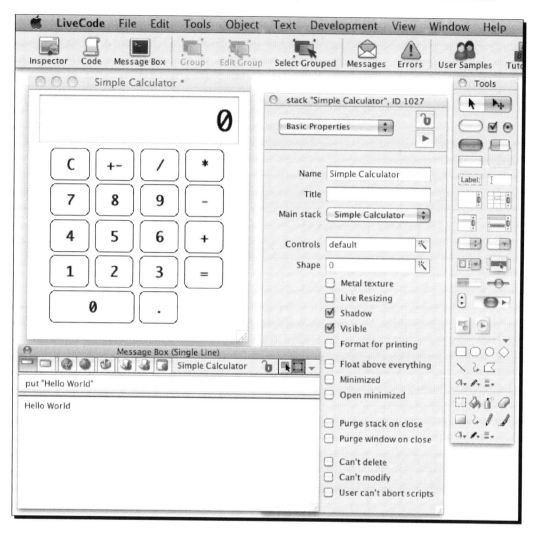

Main windows

In addition to the document window itself, these are the main windows that we will need to be familiar with for now:

- **Tools** palette
- **Inspector** palette
- **Message Box**

The upper area of the **Tools** palette shows all of the interface controls that you will need to create an interactive application. Below them are a set of tools for editing vector graphics, and a set of tools for editing bitmap graphics.

The **Inspector** palette shows all of the options for the control that you currently have selected. In the above screenshot nothing is selected, and so the **Inspector** palette is showing information about the stack itself.

The **Message Box** is a window that lets you try out either single or multiple lines of code. You will be able to invoke functions in your stacks too, making it a very handy way to test individual functions while you are tracking down issues. We'll use the **Message Box** in later chapters.

As suggested above, you should read the User Guide to get a deeper understanding of these windows, but let's try putting together something simple for now, to get you more familiar with using the **Tool** palette.

Time for action – it's a drag, but you'll like it!

You build things in LiveCode by dragging icons from the **Tools** palette to the Stack window. If the palettes are not already open, the **Inspector** palette can be opened by clicking the icon on the left-hand side end of the toolbar, or selecting one of the inspector menu items in the **Object** menu. The **Tools** palette can be opened by selecting **Tools Palette** from the **Tools** menu. To do this, perform the following steps:

1. From the **File** menu, select **New Mainstack.**

2. In the **Tools** palette, click on the **Edit** tool (the top right-hand side icon).

Select Edit, or not...

In LiveCode you can drag controls from the **Tools** palette to the card window without first selecting the **Edit** tool. However, if you are in the **Run** tool you will not be able to select the control in order to adjust its position or size, and so in these instructions we are intentionally selecting the **Edit** tool before adding controls to the card window, just to be sure.

3. Drag icons from the upper section of the **Tools** palette to the stack window.

4. Try the layering options at the bottom of the **Object** menu.

5. Select more than one item, and experiment with the **Align Objects** options in the **Inspector** palette. The align options are shown automatically when you select multiple objects, but you can also select **Align Objects** from the drop-down menu in the **Inspector** palette. You won't see that option if only one object is selected. Here we see the options, because three buttons are selected:

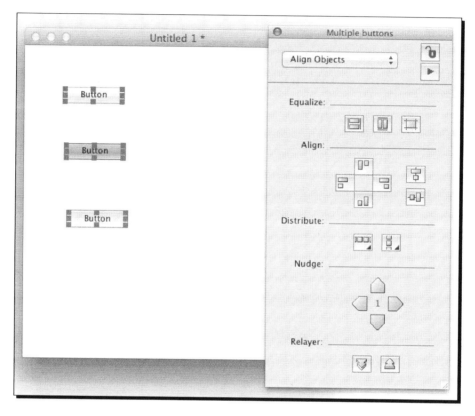

6. Select a single button, and in the **Inspector** palette enter a **Name** and a **Label**. If you don't see the name and label fields, make sure you have selected **Basic Properties** from the **Inspector** pallet's drop-down menu.

7. Add several more controls to the card window, and practice aligning and naming the controls. You can also resize them by dragging on the handles that you see on the corners and the sides, while the control is selected. Here is how it could look if you had added some buttons, a field, a tab panel, and a video player control:

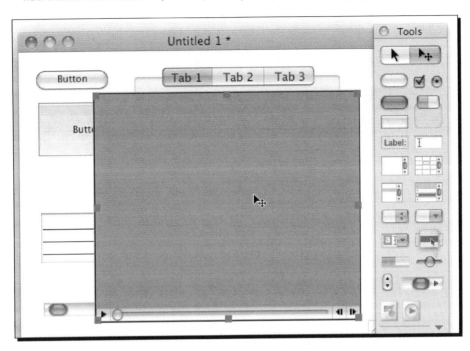

What just happened?

Hopefully you will have made a random bunch of interface controls, perhaps some that are nicely lined up too! Now delete them all, and get ready to make the simple calculator interface.

But first we should go over some of the structure and hierarchy of a LiveCode stack, and also create some basic navigation.

Creating a hierarchy

Everything goes somewhere, but having things in the wrong place can lead to problems. So we should learn more about the structure of a LiveCode stack.

Stack structure

As described in the *Background history and metaphors* section of this chapter, LiveCode uses a stack of cards metaphor. When you make a new stack you, in effect, have a single-card stack of cards. However, even the simplest application is likely to have more than one card. For example, there could be a splash screen, a title card, cards for the actual task at hand, and a credits page. In the calculator stack we will use two cards. The **Tools** menu includes an option to view the structure of the stack, by showing the **Application Browser**:

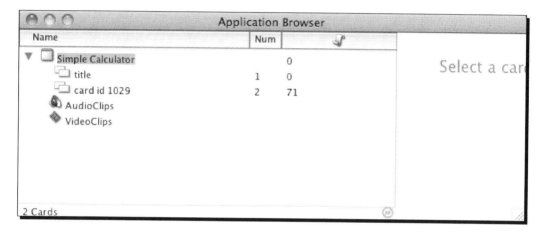

Where code goes

In programming languages like the one in LiveCode, code is referred to as **scripts**, while methods or functions are known as **handlers** (though in LiveCode a handler that returns a value is also called a function). Projects made with harder-to-use programming tools often consist of dozens of external text files, one for each model, view, or controller. In LiveCode this is simpler; the scripts are attached to the object that needs that code.

To deal with user interaction in other tools you will have to write code that receives the event (perhaps just a mouse-click on a button), and to then perform the relevant action. In LiveCode there is a message path that takes care of these events and passes them up the hierarchy. If you click on a LiveCode interface control that doesn't have a mouse event handler, the click goes up the hierarchy to the card level. If the card doesn't have a handler for that event, it continues up to the stack level.

You can have additional levels of hierarchy, by putting other stacks into use, but for our purposes we just need the button, card, and stack hierarchies.

This message hierarchy allows us to place the code needed by several interface controls into a higher level, available to all of those controls. One such case will be with the calculator's number buttons; each one needs to do exactly the same thing, and by putting that code into the card level, each of them can make use of that single handler.

to having the shared handler in the card level, or much
ou are developing the code for the simple calculator, you
d script, instead of 11 individual calculator button scripts.

ilator, and add scripts to the 14 buttons, a field,

imple code

ie example code files for all Packt books you have purchased
t http://www.packtpub.com. If you purchased this
u can visit http://www.packtpub.com/support and
files e-mailed directly to you.

ing and navigating between cards

d a title screen, but we'll make one anyway, in order to
ing some basic navigation. You can either take your cleared-out
lew **Mainstack** from the **File** menu.

m the **Object** menu.

I to either go to the previous card (**Go Prev**), or first card

/e the **Edit** tool selected in the **Tools** palette, and drag a **Label** field
he card window. In this case you can easily see which one is the
Label field (i. .., **Label:** in the icon), but as a general tip, you can point to controls
in the **Tools** palette and see a help tip that shows what kind of control it is.

4. In the **Basic Properties** section of the **Inspector** palette, uncheck the **Don't wrap** check box.

5. Type title into the **Name** entry field.

6. Choose **Contents** from the **Inspector** drop-down menu, and replace the initial text that says **Label:** by typing Simple Calculator into the contents entry field.

7. Choose **Text Formatting** from the drop-down menu, and click on the align text center button, which is the middle of the three **Align** buttons.

8. Change the **Font**, **Size**, and **Style** options, to make a nice looking title, resizing the field itself until you like how it looks:

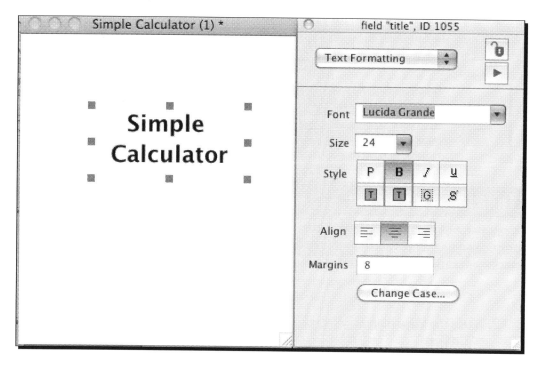

9. Drag a **Push** button (the second icon from the top left-hand side in the **Tools** palette) from the **Tools** palette, and place it below the title field.

10. In the **Inspector**, choose **Basic Properties** from the drop-down menu (it's the menu that says **Text Formatting** in the screen shot above), type in Begin into the **Name** entry field. LiveCode will automatically show the same text as the button's label, even though you didn't type it into the **Label** entry field.

11. You can go into the text formatting options for buttons too, if you wish!

12. Mentally prepare yourself - we're about to type in our first script!

13. With the button selected, choose **Object Script** from the **Object** menu. You can also right-click on the button itself, and select **Edit Script**.

14. The Script window will appear, and will show a starter script, of on mouseUp, (empty line), and end mouseUp as shown in the following screenshot:

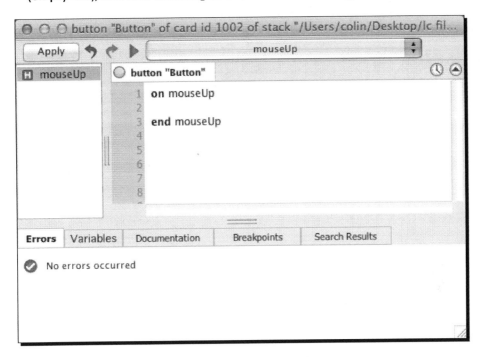

15. Complete the script by typing in go next into the blank line to give you this final script:

```
on mouseUp
go next
end mouseUp
```

16. Close the script window, and click on **Yes** when asked if you want to save the changes.

17. Choose the **Browse** tool from the **Tools** palette (the upper left-most tool, that looks like a regular cursor arrow), and click on the **Begin** button that you just made. All being well you're now looking at a blank card. Don't worry, you didn't just delete the title field and button! You're now on the second of the two cards that you made earlier. Use the **View** menu again to go back to the first card, to try the button again.

18. Save! From the **File** menu, choose **Save**, and save the stack, with the name Simple Calculator, somewhere you can easily find later. Perhaps you could make a folder to hold the stacks you will make while reading this book.

What just happened?

That may have seemed like a lot of steps, but we did create the two cards we need, laid out a nice looking title field, and created a **Begin** button with its own script. In reality those steps take under two minutes, and even less as you gain experience in LiveCode.

Pop quiz – best name?

If you want to make it big in the multimedia authoring tool world, which of these names would be a bad choice?

1. Henry
2. Bill
3. Bob
4. Kevin

Making a simple calculator application

With even a basic familiarity with LiveCode, you can start to make something of use. Here we will make a very simple calculator stack.

Inspector clues, oh...

You will find yourself using the **Inspector** palette a lot, so take a moment to study how it behaves. When you select an object on the card you will see that the **Inspector** palette changes its appearance, sometimes even its height, to show the options for the item you have selected. It is smart enough to notice when you have selected multiple items, and will then show the align tools.

Sometimes you will want to keep an **Inspector** palette set to view the options of a particular object on the card, and to not switch to show a different object as you make other selections. In the upper right-hand side corner of the **Inspector** palette is a padlock icon, which will let you lock the inspector to the current object.

So far, most of the **Inspector** palette options haven't affected us, but one that is about to be relevant is the fact that you can set a name for an item that is different to its label. You may know from other programming languages, and this also applies to LiveCode, that some names are less legal than others. Perhaps you can't have spaces in the name, or use a colon, or backslash. If you name a button with a number, Button "1" may not be Button 1, and that could lead to confusion.

For the calculator keys we will set a label to make it look correct, and a name that doesn't lead to confusion. Speaking of those calculator keys...

Time for action – making the calculator buttons

Using the first screenshot from this chapter as a guide, let's build the calculator buttons (the scripts you will type are also listed later on, if you want to make sure you typed it correctly):

1. If you're not already there, go to the second card (the currently empty one).

2. Make sure the **Edit** button is selected in the **Tools** palette, and drag a **Push** button to the card, in the position of the button with the label **7**.

3. In the **Basic Properties** of the **Inspector** palette, set the **Style** drop-down menu to **Rounded Rectangle** (in real life you would take the time to have nice graphical buttons, here you are just matching my ugly "programmer art"!).

4. Set the name of the button to `number7`, and the label to `7`.

5. Select **Object Script** from the **Object** menu to see the starter script as you did with the **Begin** button.

6. In the empty line between `on mouseUp` and `end mouseUp`, type `numberPressed the label of me`.

7. Close and save the script.

8. Select the button and make a copy of it, by choosing **Duplicate Objects** from the **Edit** menu, and position it where the button with the label **8** will be. Copy/Paste and alt-drag are two other ways to duplicate an object.

9. Set the name to `number8`, and the label to `8`.

10. Repeat steps 8 and 9, for the buttons **9, 4, 5, 6, 1, 2, 3, 0**, and the decimal point, using the corresponding number instead of **8**. For the decimal point, set the name to `decimalpoint`.

11. Duplicate one of the buttons again, name the new button `divide`, and type / for its label.

12. Select **Object Script** for the divide button, and change `numberPressed` in the middle line to `operatorPressed`, making the whole line read as `operatorPressed the short name of me`.

13. Duplicate the divide button three more times, and set the names to `multiply`, `plus`, and `minus`. Set the labels to *, +, and -.

14. Duplicate the divide button again, giving the name `equals` to the button and setting the label to =, and changing the middle line of script to say `equalsPressed`

15. Duplicate the `equals` button, and set the new button's name to `toggleSign` and label to `+-`, then change the middle line of script to `toggleSign`.

16. Duplicate the `equals` button, set the new button's name to `clear` and label to `C`, then change the middle line of script to be `clearPressed`.

17. Drag a **Label** field from the **Tools** palette, and in the **Inspector** palette choose **Text Formatting** from the drop-down menu. In the **Text Formatting** settings choose a nice looking font, right justified text, and a large font size. Name the field `display`.

18. Edit the script of the `display` field. With fields you don't get the starter script that you get with buttons, so you will need to type the mouseUp lines yourself. Type the following three lines:

```
on mouseUp
set the clipboarddata["TEXT"] to me
end mouseUp
```

19. Move all of the buttons into their right spots, and select sets of buttons to then use the Align tools to make your calculator layout match the screenshot.

20. Save!

What just happened?

Quite a lot just happened! We have now made all of the card level objects, and typed in their scripts. Most of the scripts are "calling" up to a card level handler that we will be setting up next. Before we do that it's worth trying to understand some of the lines we just entered.

Verbosity, synonyms, and "me"

The near-English nature of the programming language in LiveCode is amazingly powerful, but rigidly so. In some other tools you have a choice of whether you use verbose English-like syntax, less verbose, or what is called **dot syntax**. The **Lingo language**, in Adobe Director, is a good example to compare to.

Suppose we want to change the text inside a field that is the first entry of a Director movie's cast, we can use verbose syntax:

```
put "hello world" into the text of member 1
```

or slightly less verbose syntax:

```
the text of member 1 = "hello world"
```

or dot syntax:

```
member(1).text = "hello world"
```

In LiveCode there isn't that choice - what you type has to be in the form of:

```
put value into container
```

You do have a choice about whether you use a long version of a word, a short version, or an abbreviated form. There are also synonyms, which allow you to use a word that makes more sense to you.

Here are two ways of saying the same thing, with the second variation using an abbreviated form of the key words:

```
put character 3 of word 2 of card field "name of field 1" into
aVariable
```

```
put char 3 of word 2 of fld 1 into aVariable
```

When you are dealing with the contents of the object that has the script that is running, you can use the keyword me to save on some typing, and LiveCode will also try to work out what you have in mind, if possible.

Take the lines we have entered as examples:

```
numberPressed the label of me
```

numberPressed will propagate up to a card handler we will add (soon). the label of me will look at the Label that you set for the object that the script is inside of.

```
set the clipboarddata["TEXT"] to me
```

In this case, me would normally refer to the object (as is the case with the label of me), but because we gave the extra clue of ["TEXT"], LiveCode knows that it's the text contents of the field that has that script, and not the field itself. Still, because there is the potential for confusion when reading your own code later, you could add a couple of words to make the meaning more clear:

```
set the clipboarddata["TEXT"] to the text of me
```

> By the way, that display field script is not needed for the calculator to work. It's just there so that at any time you can click on the field and have the current value be copied to the clipboard, to paste into other applications.

You might choose to be more verbose than is needed, just for readability reasons, and in these chapters that is going to be the case. Using:

```
put the text of me into textvariable
```

makes it easier to tell what is going to happen than if you use the equally valid:

```
put me into textVariable
```

In either case, as it's a field, LiveCode knows what you meant.

Now look at the script in which we typed `short name of me` - what's that all about? Objects in LiveCode have a lengthy description of where they are located, e.g. "button "buttonname" of card id 1234 of stack "path/to/stack.livecode"". In the calculator application we need only the single word you set as the name of the button. If we asked for `name of me`, it would still say `button "buttonname"`. To just grab the name itself, we use `short name of me`.

There are times when you will want to use the other variations of "name", including the long name and the abbreviated name, which you can read about in the LiveCode Dictionary entry for "name". In addition to a description of the different ways to use "name", there are a number of cautions shown.

Case sensitivity

If any advanced LiveCode users are reading this chapter, they may notice that in some instances I have the case wrong. LiveCode doesn't mind what case you have used, and so when I incorrectly said `clipboarddata` instead of `clipboardData`, it didn't matter. This isn't unique to LiveCode, but it is common amongst English-like programming languages to not demand that the user gets the case exactly right before the command will work.

Adding the card handlers

If you had dared to try using the calculator buttons, you would have seen a lot of script errors. We need to add in the card level handlers to be at the receiving end of the calls that the buttons are making. Instead of walking you through typing one line of code at a time, it would probably be quicker to present the lines in one go and explain what each line does. As a practice run, here are the lines that we have entered so far:

On all of the number buttons and the decimal point button, you should have this script:

```
on mouseup
   numberPressed the label of me
end mouseup
```

on mouseUp is triggered when you press and release the left mouse button while on the button, numberPressed will call a card handler named "numberPressed", passing with it the Label that you had set for the button that holds this script.

The C (clear) button has this script:

```
on mouseUp
    clearPressed
end mouseUp
```

clearPressed will call a card script named "clearPressed"

The other buttons all work in much the same way - they call a handler of the name used, which we're about to add to the card script. The following is the script for the +, -, *, and / buttons, passing the name of the button in question to the card level:

```
on mouseUp
    operatorPressed the short name of me
end mouseUp
```

And this is the one on the +- button:

```
on mouseUp
    toggleSign
end mouseUp
```

The display field has this script:

```
on mouseUp
    set the clipboarddata["TEXT"] to me
end mouseUp
```

In the case of the field, it's only processing one line of code, so no need to put that up on the card level, unless we had a lot of fields doing the same thing.

So, why don't we add all those card level scripts? Here they are, one at a time, with an explanation of how each one works:

But wait... we haven't yet talked about variables. Hold that thought, while we see how LiveCode handles variables.

Variable types in LiveCode

Generally speaking, variables are memory locations where you store values that you need to access later. In most programming languages you can dictate which routines have access to which variables. Less English-like languages may use the terms "public", "private", and "protected". Things are not all that different in LiveCode but here the words used describe more the region where the variable can be used. If a variable is to be readable everywhere, it would be "global". If it's just to be used in the current script, it's "local".

LiveCode also has custom property variables, and many people would use those for the calculator button values instead of relying on the label of the button. We'll perhaps use them later!

Now, where was I... oh yes, card level scripts:

This is the first line of the card script:

```
global currenttotal,currentvalue,currentcommand,newnumber
```

As we just discussed, these are variables that will allow all of the handlers to pass values to each other. In this case the variables could have been `local`, but you may often decide to use `global` instead, thinking that a case may come up later where you need to access the variables from outside the script you're in.

It's good to reset things when you first start, and LiveCode has an `opencard` event that we can use to do this. The following code resets things:

```
on opencard
   clearpressed
end opencard

on clearpressed
   put true into newnumber
   put 0 into field "display"
   put 0 into currenttotal
   put 0 into currentvalue
   put empty into currentcommand
end clearpressed
```

Having the reset lines in the `clearPressed` handler will allow us to call it at other times and not just when the card opens. We can call it directly when clicking on the `C` (clear) button which will zero out the display field, the running total for your calculation, and the last number that you entered into the calculator. It also clears the variable that is used to remember which operator button you last pressed, and a boolean (true/false) variable used to recognize whether a number button you press should clear the display or append to the display.

All of the numbered buttons, and the decimal point button, call this handler:

```
on numberPressed n
    if newnumber is true then
        put n into field "display"
        put false into newnumber
    else
        put n after field "display"
    end if
end numberPressed
```

The n after the handler name is a parameter variable that stores what was sent to the handler. In this case it's the label of the button that was pressed. All this routine needs to do is add the character to the end of the display field, except for when you are typing in a new number. That's where the newNumber boolean variable comes in - if that is set to true, the incoming character replaces the contents of the display field. However, if it's false, the character is added to the end of the field.

This is the handler for when you press the +, -, *, or / buttons:

```
on operatorPressed operator
    if currentCommand is empty then
        put field "display" into currentTotal
        put operator into currentCommand
        put true into newNumber
    else
        put operator into currentCommand
        equalsPressed
    end if
end operatorPressed
```

When you use a calculator, you type in a number, an operator, and then another number, followed by either another operator or the = button. At the time you press the operator button there is no way to know the result, as you haven't yet entered the next number in the calculation. So, we remember the operator till you have entered the next number. If the currentcommand variable doesn't already have a value, we store the display field text into the currenttotal variable, the operator character that you pressed into the currentcommand variable, and make sure that newnumber is set to true. Doing this makes sure that the next number button you press will clear the display field. If currentcommand already has a value, we replace it with the new value, and then call the same handler that is used when you press the = button.

There are most likely shorter ways to deal with the = button being pressed, but here we'll use several `if` statements, and run the appropriate calculation code:

```
on equalsPressed
   put field "display" into currentValue
   if currentCommand is empty then exit equalsPressed
   if currentCommand is "divide" then put currentTotal / currentValue
into field "display"
   if currentCommand is "multiply" then put currentTotal *
currentValue into field "display"
   if currentCommand is "minus" then put currentTotal - currentValue
into field "display"
   if currentCommand is "plus" then put currentTotal + currentValue
into field "display"
   put field "display" into currentTotal
   put true into newNumber
   put empty into currentCommand
end equalsPressed
```

The contents of the display field are stored in the `currentValue` variable, and the last operator button you pressed (that is stored in `currentCommand`) is looked at, to see what happens next. If there wasn't a previous operator (as would be the case if you pressed = twice in a row) we ignore the button press and exit the routine. For the four operators, we do the appropriate calculation. Afterwards, we store the new running total into the `currentTotal` variable, make sure that the `newNumber` boolean variable is set to `true` (so that the next number button pressed will clear the display field), and we forget the last operator button that was pressed, by putting `empty` into the `currentCommand` variable.

One thing to note is that LiveCode is smart enough to know that the text string inside the display field is to be treated as a floating point number.

For the last handler, `togglesign`, insert the following code:

```
on togglesign
   if character 1 of field "display" is "-" then
      delete character 1 of field "display"
   else
      put "-" before field "display"
   end if
end togglesign
```

This is a very simple routine, that doesn't have to understand that it's floating point numbers being represented. It simply looks to see if the first character is a minus or not, and if it is, it deletes the character. If not, it inserts the hyphen that LiveCode will later interpret as a negative value.

Pop quiz – try to remember...

As you get to learn a new tool you can end up taking a lot of time remembering where the thing is that you need. You know what you want to do, you know how to do it, but you can't remember where that thing is located! Where did you go to set the text styling for the calculator's title field?

1. The **Edit** menu.
2. The **Object** menu.
3. The **Text Formatting** section of the **Inspector** palette.
4. The **Text** menu.

Extending the calculator

It is possible to add more features to the simple calculator. If we consider how the buttons are named, and the functions in the card script, you can start to see what would be involved in adding a new ability:

♦ The calculator operator buttons are named so that the card script knows which one you clicked on.

♦ When the = button is pressed, there are a set of `if` statements in the `equalspressed` handler that determine what happens next.

Have a go hero – getting to the root of things

On Windows you can make a square root symbol with *Alt+251*, and on Mac with *Option+v*. Unfortunately LiveCode doesn't like those as button labels! At least on Mac, when you type that character into the **Inspector** palette, the character immediately vanishes. One workaround would be to use the message box, and type this:

```
set the label of btn "squareroot" to "√"
```

That should give you the right symbol as the button label.

LiveCode has a square root function; typing this into the **Message Box** would produce the square root of 10:

```
put sqrt(10)
```

Now, armed with the above information, try to add a square root feature to the calculator.

Other interface controls

So far we have only had to look at buttons and fields to be able to create the calculator. In later chapters we will use many more controls, so let's take a sneak peek at those.

Video player control

If your system has QuickTime installed, LiveCode can play QuickTime movies, using the Player control type. Those can be added to the card in several ways, as well as by using a script command as described in the following points:

- A file can be added from your hard drive by selecting **Import as Control/Video File** from the **File** menu
- An empty player can be created by selecting **New Control/Player** from the **Object** menu
- A player control can be dragged from the **Tools** palette to the card
- A player can be created with code, including setting its name:

```
new player "player name"
```

Having added the player to the card, you can then set which video file is to be played by entering the file path or URL of the file under the **Basic Settings** of the **Inspector** palette. You can also set the path to the video with the following script:

```
set the filename of player "player name" to "file path or URL"
```

Still image control

In the same way that you just saw for playing video, still images can also be added to a stack. All of the options shown for adding a video player can be used for images. Here, for example, is the script needed to add the RunRev company logo to the card:

```
new image "revlogo"
set the filename of image "revlogo" to "http://www.runrev.com/runrev-
globals/corporate-nav/images/runrev.gif"
```

Rollover buttons

Images that you import can be used as icons in a button. To set up a button so that it has a nice idle state image, and an associated highlight image, you would do the following steps:

1. Select **File | Import As Control | Image File...**
2. Choose the images that represent the idle and highlight states, and click on **Open**.

3. Select the button that you wish to look like these images, and under I**cons & Border** in the **Inspector** palette, click on the magic wand button to the right-hand side of the top entry (**Icon**).

4. In the dialog that appears, select **This Stack** from the drop-down menu.

5. Select the image that is the idle state for the button.

6. Click on the magic wand button next to the **Hover** entry, and choose the highlight state image.

7. Under **Basic Properties**, choose **Transparent Button** from the **Style** drop-down menu.

8. Uncheck the boxes for **Show name**, **Auto hilite**, and **Shared hilite**.

9. Resize the button to be big enough to show the image.

10. Select each of the original images, and under **Basic Properties**, uncheck the **Visible** box.

Here we can see two images that have been imported in order to give the **Begin** button a more iOS appearance. The button is selected, and the **Inspector** palette shows the icon selection choices.

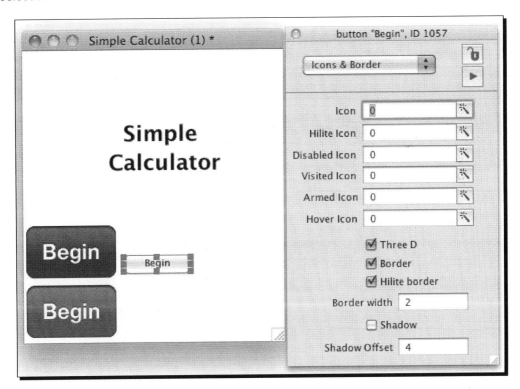

Then when you choose an image to use, the button itself will be updated. In this case the **Hover Icon** has been set to the darker version of the graphic, but as shown here, the button still needs to be resized.

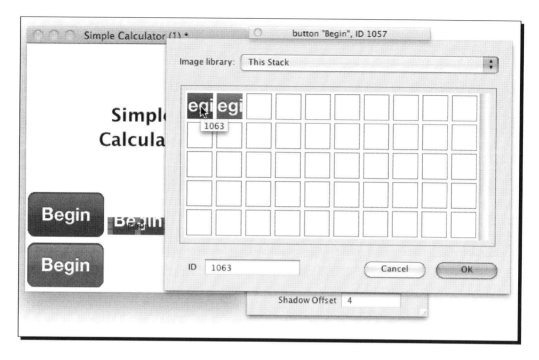

Many More Controls...

LiveCode has a lot of different controls. Many are just slight variations, but there are plenty that are quite different from each other. Look at the **Object** menu, and then **New Control**. As you'll see the list is very long!

Debugging

If you did go ahead and try the calculator before we had entered all the scripts it needed, you most likely would have got to see the script debugging in action. Hopefully you managed to cope with what you saw; it can be overwhelming at first. The following screenshot is what it would have looked like:

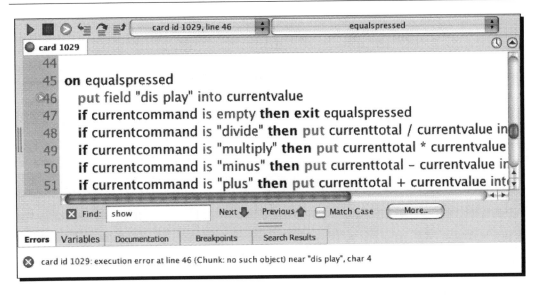

Most of what you see is the same as when you edit scripts, but if you do see the debug variation you are actually in a paused state, a freeze frame of the program as it runs. In this example the program stopped because line 46 is looking for a field named dis play, and there isn't such a field, it should be display.

The error message at the bottom makes it clear that the error is something to do with the field name, and you would quickly spot the typo. Sometimes though you may need to inspect the variables, to make sure they contain the values you think they should. The **Variables** tab will show a list of those.

An unexpected problem is the one time you may see the debugger, but when developing a script you are able to set **Breakpoints** by clicking in the column just to the left-hand side of the line number you want to halt the program at.

Once the script is halted by a breakpoint, you can use the row of buttons at the top to step through the code. Those buttons are:

- **Continue** will set the script running again
- **Stop** will stop the script running, so that you can make changes
- **Show next statement** will show an indicator to the left-hand side of the current line
- **Step into next statement** is used for stepping into a different handler

- **Step over next statement** will go onto the next statement in the current handler, without stepping into a handler mentioned on the current line

- **Step out of current handler** is used to skip the remaining lines in a handler that you had previously stepped into, and exit back out to the handler that called the current one

You will become more familiar with the script editor and debugger as you go along, but that should get you started!

RunRev's online tutorials

In this chapter we have covered just enough to make you familiar with the environment, to practice using some controls, and to do a little script writing. There is quite a lot to LiveCode as a tool, and so you may be interested in looking into other topics, or going into more depth than is covered here.

A good starting point would be RunRev's own set of online tutorials, which are located in the following location:

```
http://lessons.runrev.com/
```

Type into the search box words that describe your area of interest, and you will see a list of articles on that topic.

Summary

Having created a simple calculator from scratch, you should now be more familiar with the LiveCode environment.

In this chapter we covered:

- Buttons, fields, scripts, and stack structure, to get an understanding of how they work together.

- Several short scripts, to illustrate the English-like syntax used by LiveCode.

- The script window, and how you would debug a script.

- Other interface controls, in preparation for using them in later chapters.

We also discussed the kinds of variables used by LiveCode, and how it can use abbreviated commands and synonyms.

Now that we've learned enough to make regular LiveCode stacks, we need to download and install additional software from Google and Apple that is required for publishing a stack to a mobile device, and then begin to try out mobile specific features, both of which are covered in the next chapter.

2
Getting Started with LiveCode Mobile

Before we can do neat things...

Creating stacks that do something that you will find useful or that may become a mobile app that you can sell, is a very gratifying process. Minute by minute, you can be making progress, and instantly see improvements that you have made. Unfortunately, there is a lot of less gratifying work to be done before and after you have made your masterpiece. This chapter will take you through the "before" part.

LiveCode makes mobile apps by taking the stack you have made, along with any supporting files you have added, and compiles the application file using the developer kit that you will download from the mobile OS provider – Google for Android and Apple for iOS.

In this chapter we will:

- ◆ Sign up for Android Market
- ◆ Sign up for Amazon Appstore
- ◆ Download and install the Android SDK
- ◆ Configure LiveCode so that it knows where to look for the Android SDK
- ◆ Become an iOS developer with Apple
- ◆ Download and install Xcode
- ◆ Configure LiveCode so that it knows where to look for the iOS SDKs
- ◆ Set up simulators and physical devices
- ◆ Test a stack in a simulator and physical device

Here we go...

iOS, Android, or both?

It could be that you only have an interest in iOS or only in Android. You should be able to easily see where to skip ahead to, unless you're intrigued about how the other half lives! If, like me, you're a capitalist, then you should be interested in both OSes.

Far fewer steps are needed to get the Android SDK than to get the iOS developer tools, because of having to sign up as a developer with Apple, but the configuration for Android is more involved. We'll go through all the steps for Android and then the ones for iOS. If you're an iOS-only kind of person, skip the next few pages, picking up again at the *Becoming an iOS Developer* section.

Becoming an Android developer

It is possible to develop Android OS apps without having to sign up for anything, but we'll try to be optimistic and assume that within the next 12 months, you will find time to make an awesome app that will make you rich! To that end, we'll go over what is involved in signing up to publish your apps in both the Android Market and the Amazon Appstore.

Android Market

A good starting location would be `http://developer.android.com/`.

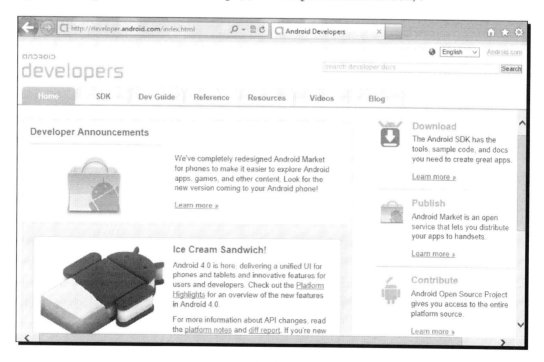

You will be back here shortly to download the Android SDK, but for now, click on the **Learn More** link in the **Publish** area. There will be a sign-in screen; sign in using your usual Google details.

Which e-mail address to use?

Some Google services are easier to sign up for, if you have a Gmail account. Creating a Google+ account, or signing up for some of their Cloud services, requires a Gmail address (or so it seemed to me at the time!). If you have previously set up Google Checkout as part of your account, some of the steps in signing up process become simpler. So, use your Gmail address, and if you don't have one, create one!

◆ Google charges a $25 fee for you to sign up for Android Market. At least you find out about this right away! Enter the values for **Developer Name**, **Email Address**, **Website URL** (if you have one), and **Phone Number**.

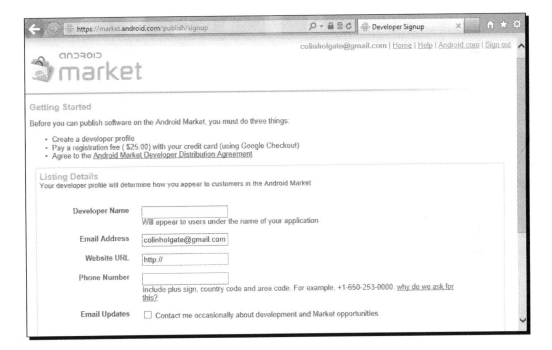

◆ The payment of the $25 can be done through **Google Checkout**.

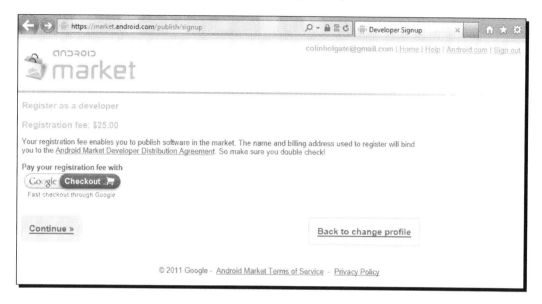

◆ Using **Google Checkout** saves you from having to enter in your billing details, each time. Hopefully you won't guess the other 12 digits of my credit card number!

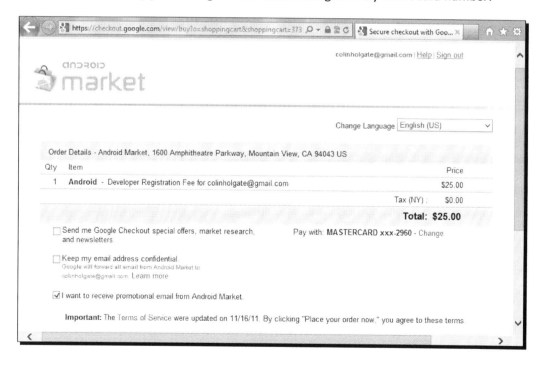

◆ Finally, you need to agree to the **Android Market Developer Distribution Agreement**.

◆ You're given an excuse to go and make some coffee...

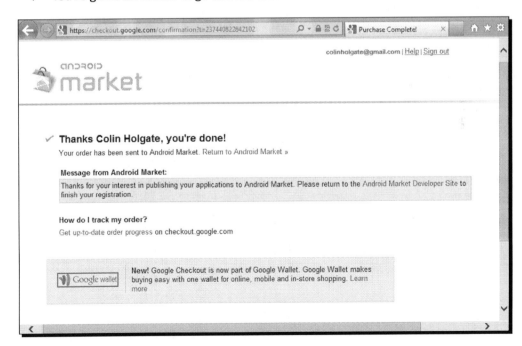

◆ Some time later, you're all signed up and ready to make your fortune!

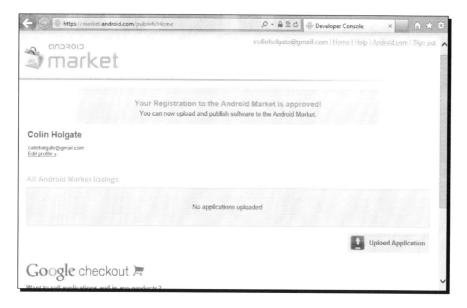

Amazon Appstore

Whereas the rules and costs for the Google Android Market are fairly relaxed, Amazon has taken a more Apple-like approach, both in the amount they charge you to register and in the review process for accepting app submissions. The starting page is `http://developer.amazon.com/home.html`.

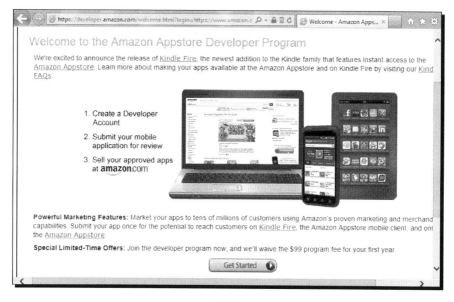

1. When you click on **Get Started**, you will be asked to sign into your Amazon account.

Which e-mail address to use?

This feels like déjà vu! There is no real advantage in using your Google e-mail address when signing up for the Amazon Appstore Developer Program, but if you happen to have an account with Amazon, sign in with that one. It will simplify the payment stage, and your developer account and general Amazon account will be associated with each other.

2. You are asked to agree to the **APPSTORE DISTRIBUTION AGREEMENT** terms before learning about the costs.

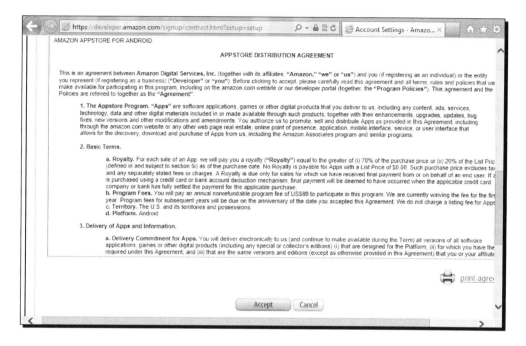

3. Those costs are $99 per year, but the first year is free. So that's good!

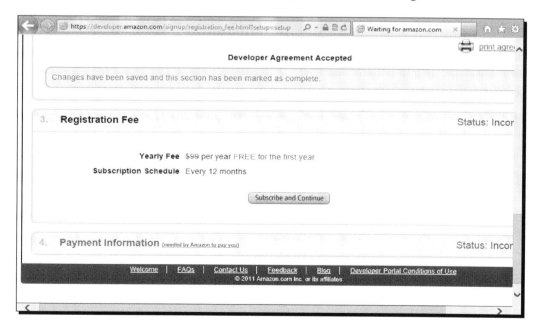

4. Unlike the Google Android Market, Amazon asks for your bank details upfront, ready to send you lots of money later, we hope!

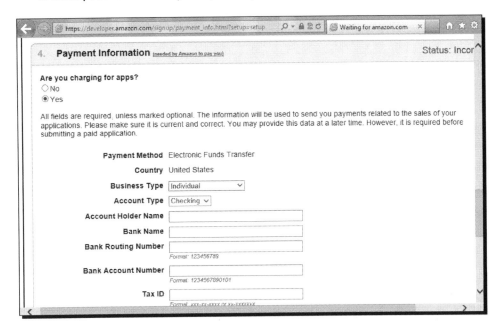

5. That's it; you're ready to make another fortune, to go along with the one that Google sends you!

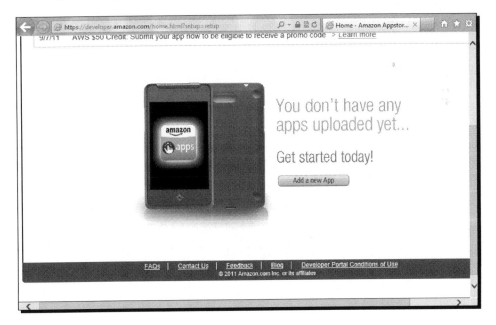

Pop quiz – when is something too much?

1. You're at the end of developing your mega-app; it's at 49.5 MB in size, and you just need to add title screen music. Why would you not add that two-minute epic tune you have lined up?

    a. It would take too long to load

    b. People tend to skip the title screen soon anyway

    c. The file size is going to go over 50 MB

    d. Heavy metal might not be appropriate for a children's storybook app

Downloading the Android SDK

Head back over to `http://developer.android.com/`, and click on the **Download** link, or go straight to `http://developer.android.com/sdk/index.html`.

Download the Android SDK

Welcome Developers! If you are new to the Android SDK, please read the steps below, for an overview of how to set up the SDK.

If you're already using the Android SDK, you should update to the latest tools or platform using the *Android SDK and AVD Manager*, rather than downloading a new SDK starter package. See Adding SDK Components.

Platform	Package	Size	MD5 Checksum
Windows	android-sdk_r15-windows.zip	33895447 bytes	cc2aadf7120d12b574981461736a96e9
	installer_r15-windows.exe (Recommended)	33902520 bytes	ee8481cb86a6646a4d963d5142902c5c
Mac OS X (intel)	android-sdk_r15-macosx.zip	30469921 bytes	03d2cdd3565771e8c7a438f1c40cc8a5
Linux (i386)	android-sdk_r15-linux.tgz	26124434 bytes	f529681fd1eda11c6e1e1d44b42c1432

In this book, we're only going to cover Windows and Mac OS X (Intel), and only as much as is needed to make LiveCode work with the Android and iOS SDKs. If you intend to do native Java-based applications, then you may be interested in reading through all of the steps that are described in the web page: `http://developer.android.com/sdk/installing.html`.

Click on the **Download** link for your platform. The steps you'll have to go through are different for Mac and Windows. Let's start with Mac.

Installing Android SDK on Mac OS X (Intel)

LiveCode itself doesn't require an Intel Mac; you can develop stacks using a PowerPC-based Mac, but both the Android SDK and some of the iOS tools require an Intel-based Mac, which sadly means that if you're reading this as you sit next to your Mac G4 or G5, then you're not going to get too far!

The file that you just downloaded will automatically expand to show a folder named `android-sdk-macosx`. It may be in your downloads folder right now; a more natural place for it would be in your Documents folder, so move it there before performing the next steps.

There is an SDK `Readme` text file that lists the steps you will need to take. If those steps are different to what we have here, then follow the steps in the `Readme`, in case they have been updated since the steps shown here were written.

Open the application Terminal, which is in `Applications/Utilities`. You need to change the directories to be located in the `android-sdk-macosx` folder. One handy trick in Terminal is that you can drag the items into the Terminal window to get the file path to that item. Using that trick, you can type `cd` and a space into the Terminal window, then drag the `android-sdk-macosx` folder just after the space character. You'll end up with this line:

```
new-host-3:~ colin$ cd /Users/colin/Documents/android-sdk-macosx
```

Of course, the first part of the line and the `user` folder will match yours, not mine! The rest will look the same. Here's how it would look for a user named `fred`:

```
new-host-3:~ fred$ cd /Users/fred/Documents/android-sdk-macosx
```

Whatever your name is, press the *Return* or *Enter* key after entering that line. The location line changes to look similar to the following:

```
new-host-3:android-sdk-macosx colin$
```

Either type carefully or copy and paste this line from the read me file:

```
tools/android update sdk --no-ui
```

Press *Return* or *Enter* again. How long the downloads take will depend on your Internet connection. Even with a very fast Internet connection, it will still take over an hour.

Installing Android SDK on Windows

The downloads page recommends using the `exe` download link, and that will do extra things, such as check whether you have the **Java Development Kit (JDK)** installed. When you click on the link, use either the **Run** or **Save** options as you would with any download of a Windows installer. Here we opted to use **Run**. If you do use **Save**, then you will need to open the file after it has saved to your hard drive. In the following case, as the JDK wasn't installed, a dialog box appears saying to go to Oracle's site to get the JDK:

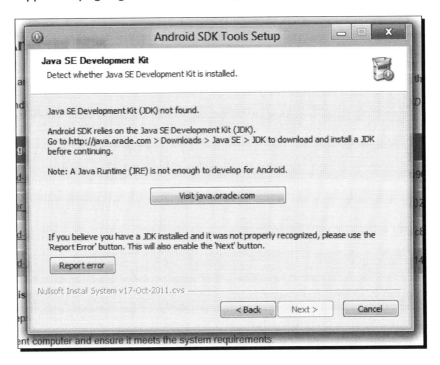

If you see this, then you can leave the dialog box open and click on the **Visit java.oracle.com** button. On the Oracle page, you have to click on a checkbox to agree to their terms, and then on the **Download** link that corresponds with your platform. Choose the **64-bit** option if you are running a 64-bit version of Windows, or the **x86** option if you are running 32-bit Windows.

Either way, you're greeted with another installer to **Run** or **Save**, as you prefer. Naturally, it takes a while for that installer to do its thing too! When the installation completes, you will see a JDK registration page; it's up to you if you register or not.

Back at the Android SDK installer dialog box, you can click on the Back button, and then the **Next** button to get back to that JDK checking stage; only now it sees that you have the JDK installed. Complete the remaining steps of the SDK installer, as you would with any Windows installer.

One important thing to notice; the last screen of the installer offers to open the SDK Manager. You do want to do that, so resist the temptation to uncheck that box!

Click on **Finish**, and you'll be greeted with a command-line window for a few moments, then the **Android SDK Manager** will appear and do its thing.

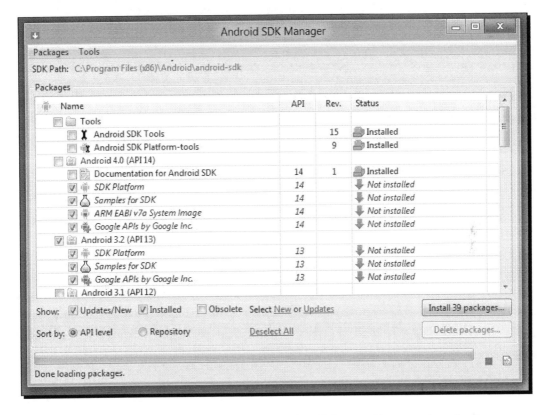

As with the Mac version, it takes a very long time for all these add-ons to download.

Pointing LiveCode to the Android SDK

After all that installation and command-line work, it's a refreshing change to get back into LiveCode!

Open the LiveCode **Preferences**, and choose **Mobile Support**.

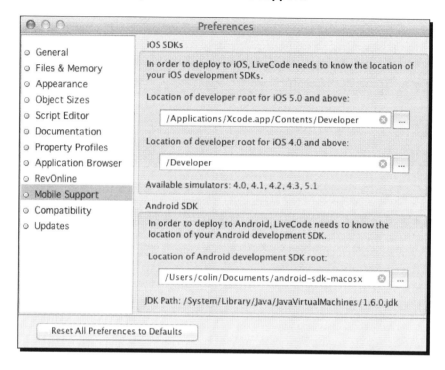

We will set the two iOS entries after getting iOS going (on Mac that is, these options will be grayed out on Windows). For now, click on the **...** button next to the Android development SDK root field, and navigate to where the SDK has been installed. If you followed the earlier steps correctly, then it will be in the `Documents` folder on Mac, or in `C:\Program Files (x86)\Android\` on Windows (or somewhere else if you chose to use a custom location).

Phew! Now, let's do iOS...

Pop quiz – tasty code names

1. Android OS uses some curious code names for each version. At the time of writing, we're on Android OS 4, which had a code name of **Ice Cream Sandwich**. Version 4.1, introduced at Google I/O in 2012, is **Jelly Bean**, and the following version is thought to be **Key Lime Pie**. Which of these is most likely to be the code name for the subsequent Android OS?

    a. Log Cabin

    b. Lunch Box

    c. Munchies

    d. Lemon Cheesecake

Becoming an iOS developer

Creating iOS LiveCode applications requires that LiveCode must have access to the iOS SDK. This is installed as a part of the Xcode developer tools, and that is a Mac-only program. Also, when you do upload an app to the iOS App Store, the application that is used is also Mac-only, and is also part of the Xcode installation. If you are a Windows-based developer and wish to develop and publish for iOS, then you will need either a virtual machine that can run Mac OS, or an actual Mac.

The biggest difference between becoming an Android developer and an iOS developer is that you have to sign up with Apple for their developer program, even if you never produce an app for the iOS App Store. If things go well, and you end up making an app for the various stores, then this isn't such a big deal. It will have cost you $25 to be able to submit to the Android Market, $99 a year (with the first year free) to submit to the Amazon Appstore, and $99 a year (including the first year) to be an iOS developer with Apple. Just sell more than 300 copies of your amazing $0.99 app, and it's paid for itself!

Your starting point for iOS is `http://developer.apple.com/programs/ios/`.

When signing up to be an iOS developer, there are four possibilities when it comes to your current status. If you already have an Apple ID, that you might use with your Apple online store purchases, or perhaps your iTunes Store purchases, then you could choose the **I already have an Apple ID...** option. In order to illustrate all of the steps in signing up, we will choose to start as a brand new user.

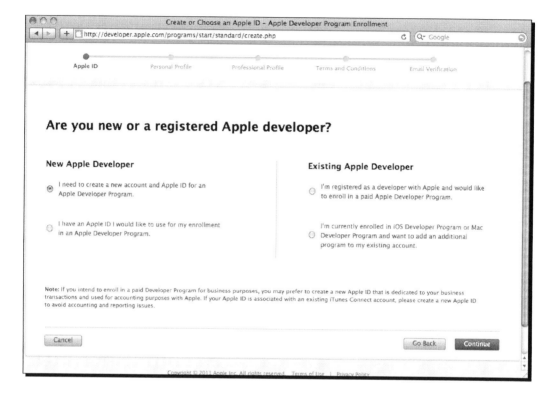

You can choose to sign up as an individual or as a company. We will choose **Individual**.

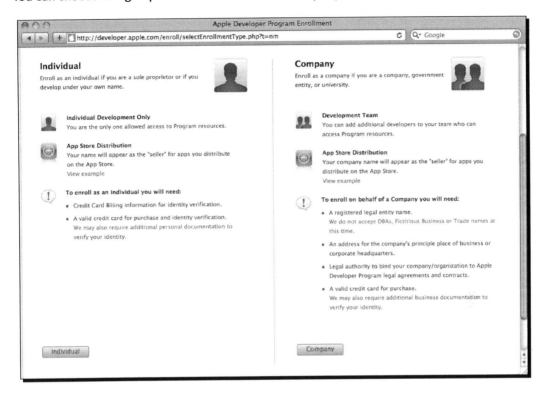

As with any such sign-up process, you will need to enter your personal details, set a security question, and enter your postal address.

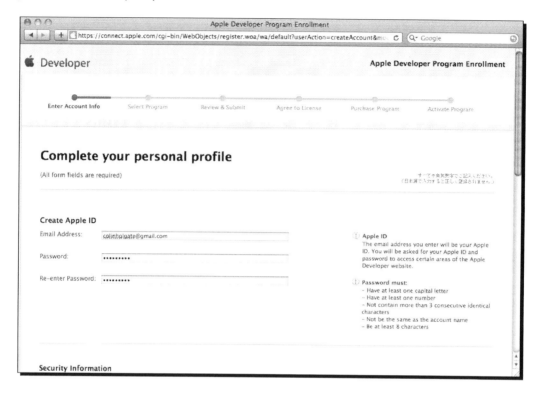

Most Apple software and services have their own legal agreement for you to sign. This one is the general **Registered Apple Developer Agreement**.

In order to verify the e-mail address you have used, a verification e-mail is sent to you, with a link in the e-mail to click on, or you can enter the code manually. Once you have completed the verification step, you can enter your billing details.

It could be that you will go on to make LiveCode applications for the Mac App Store, in which case you would also need to add the Mac Developer Program product. For our purposes, we only need to sign up for **iOS Developer Program**.

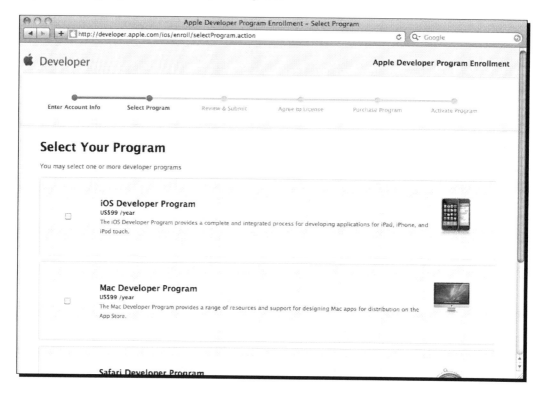

Each product that you sign up for has its own agreement. Lots of small print to read!

The actual purchasing of the iOS developer account is handled through the Apple Store for your region.

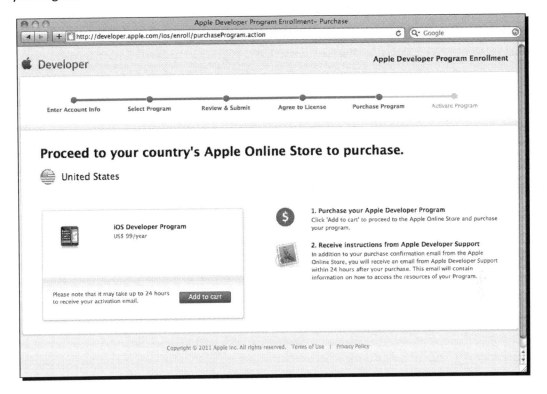

As you will see, it is going to cost you $99 per year, or $198 per year if you also signed up for the Mac Developer account. Most LiveCode users won't need to sign up for the Mac Developer account, unless the plan is to also submit desktop apps to the Mac App Store.

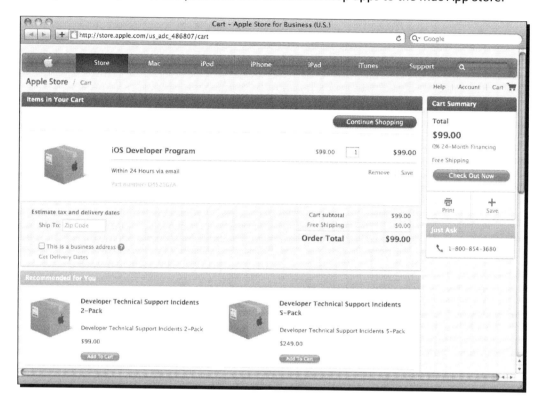

After submitting the order, you are rewarded by being told that you are now registered as an Apple Developer!

Sadly, it's not an instant approval, as was the case with the Android Market or Amazon Appstore. You have up to five days to wait for the approval. In the early iPhone Developer days, it could take a month or more, so 24 hours is an improvement!

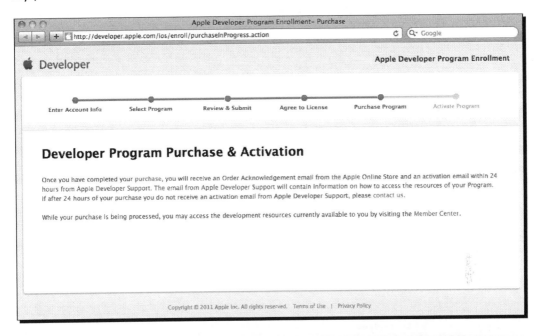

Pop quiz – iOS code names

You had it easy with the pop quiz about Android OS code names! Not so with iOS.

1. Which of these names is more likely to be a code name for a future version of iOS?

    a. Las Vegas

    b. Laguna Beach

    c. Hunter Mountain

    d. Death Valley

Installing Xcode

Once you receive the confirmation of being an iOS developer, you will be able to log into the iOS Dev Center, at `https://developer.apple.com/devcenter/ios/index.action`.

This same page is used by iOS developers who are not using LiveCode, and is full of support documents to help someone create native applications using Xcode and Objective-C. We don't need most of that, but we do need to download Xcode.

In the downloads area of the iOS Dev Center page, you will see different Xcode versions for Mac OS 10.6 (Snow Leopard) and for Mac OS 10.7 (Lion), as well as the link to the older Xcode 3. You can also get code from the Mac App Store, and as of version 4.3 of Xcode, that takes the form of an application instead of a developer folder.

Installing Xcode from the Mac App Store is very straightforward; it's just like buying any other app from the store, except that it's free! It does require that you are using Mac OS 10.7.3 or later. If you are using an older system, then you would download one of the older versions from the developer page.

The older Xcode installation process is much like any other Mac application:

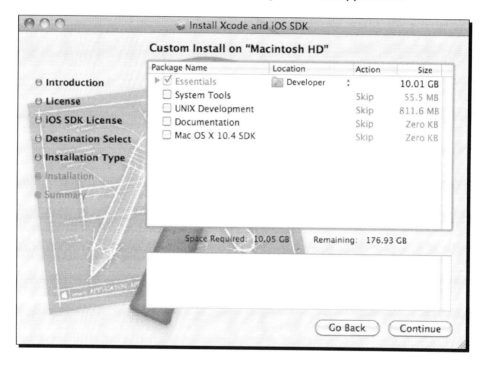

The Xcode installations take a very long time, but in the end, you should have the `Developer` folder, or new Xcode application, ready for LiveCode to find.

Coping with newer and older devices

In early 2012, Apple brought to market a new iPad. The main selling point of this one compared to the iPad 2 is that it has a "Retina" display. The regular iPads have a resolution of `1024x768`, and the Retina version has a resolution of `2048x1536`. If you wish to build applications to take advantage of that, you must get the version of Xcode from the Mac App Store, and not one of the older versions from the developer page. The new Xcode demands that you be on Mac OS 10.7.3, or later. So, to fully support the latest devices, you may have to update your system software more than you were expecting! But wait, there's more. By taking a later version of Xcode, you are then missing the iOS SDK versions that are needed to support older iOS devices, such as the original iPhone and the iPhone 3G. Fortunately, you can go into **Preferences** in Xcode, and there is a **Downloads** tab, where you can have those older SDKs downloaded into the new version of Xcode.

Pointing LiveCode to the iOS SDKs

Open the LiveCode **Preferences**, and choose **Mobile Support**.

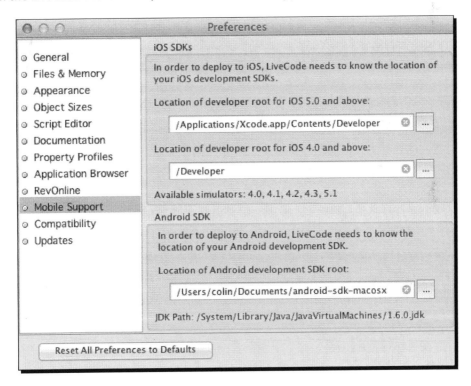

Click on the ... button next to the **Location of developer root for iOS 5.0 and above:** field, and you will see a dialog box that asks if you are using Xcode 4.2 or 4.3. If you choose 4.2, then go on to select the folder named `Developer` at the root of your hard drive. For 4.3, choose the Xcode application itself, in your `Applications` folder. If you are using an older system that wasn't able to run Xcode 4.2 or 4.3, and had to take the Xcode 3 download, click on the ... button next to the **Location of developer root for iOS 4.0 and above:** field, and again, select the folder named `Developer` at the root of your hard drive. LiveCode now knows where to find the SDKs for iOS.

Before we can make our first mobile app

Now that the required SDKs are installed, and LiveCode knows where they are, we can make a stack and test it in a simulator or on a physical device. We do, however, have to get the simulators and physical devices warmed up...

Getting ready to test for Android

Simulating on iOS is easier than it is for Android, and testing on a physical device is easier on Android than on iOS, but the setting up of physical Android devices can be horrendous!

Time for action – starting an Android virtual device

You will have to do a little digging deep into the Android SDK folders to find the Android Virtual Device setup program, and you might well want to make a shortcut or alias to it for quicker access.

1. Navigate to the Android SDK `tools` folder, located at `C:\Program Files (x86)\Android\android-sdk\` on Windows, and in your `Documents:android-sdk-macosx:tools` folder on Mac.

2. Open **AVD Manager** on Windows, or **Android** on Mac (it looks like a Unix executable - just double-click on it, and the application will open via a command-line window).

3. If you're on Mac, select **Manage AVDs...** from the **Tools** menu.

4. Select **Tablet** from the list of devices (there are only two when you have first installed the android SDK - you can add your own custom ones here as well).

5. Click on the **Start** button.

6. Sit patiently while the virtual device starts up!

7. Open LiveCode, and create a new **Mainstack**, and **Save** the stack to your hard drive.

8. Select **File | Standalone Application Settings....**

9. Click on the **Android** icon, and select the **Build for Andoid** check box.

10. Close the **Settings** dialog box, and take a look at the **Development** menu.

11. If the virtual machine is up and running, you should see it listed in the **Test Target** submenu.

What just happened?

You have opened up an Android virtual device, and LiveCode will be able to test the stacks using that device, once it has finished loading.

Connecting a physical Android device

Connecting a physical Android device can be extremely straightforward:

1. Connect your device by USB.

2. Look at the **Development Test Target** submenu to see it listed.

There can be problem cases though, and Google Search will become your best friend before you are done! We should look at an example problem case to give you ideas on how to solve any similar situations you may encounter.

Using a Kindle Fire

When it comes to finding Android devices, the Android SDK recognizes a lot of them automatically. Some devices are not recognized, and you have to do something to help **Android Debug Bridge (ADB)** find them.

ADB is the part of the Android SDK that acts as a go-between from your device to any software that needs to be able to access the device. In some cases, you will need to go into the Android system on the device to tell it to allow access for development purposes. For example, on an Android 3 (Honeycomb) device, you need to go into **Settings | Applications | Development**, and activate the USB debugging mode.

Kindle Fire comes with USB debugging already enabled; you don't have to do anything, but the ADB system doesn't know about the device at all. You can fix that!

Time for action – adding a Kindle Fire to ADB

It only takes one line of text to add the Kindle Fire to the list of devices that ADB knows about. The harder part is tracking down the text file to edit, and getting ADB to restart after making the changes. Things are more involved with Windows than Mac, because you also have to configure the USB driver, so the two systems are shown here as separate processes:

For Windows:

1. In Windows Explorer, navigate to where the file `adb_usb.ini` is located, at `C:\Users\yourusername\.android\`.

2. Open the text file `adb_usb.ini` in a text editor. The file has no visible line breaks, so Wordpad would be a better option than Notepad.

3. On the line after the three instruction lines, type `0x1949`.

4. Make sure there are no blank lines, and the last character in the text file should be the `9` at the end of `0x1949`.

5. Save.

6. Navigate to where `android_winusb.inf` is located, at `C:\Program Files (x86)\Android\android-sdk\extras\google\usb_driver\`.

7. Right-click on the file, and in **Properties | Security**, select **Users** from the list, and click on **Edit** to set the permissions so that you are allowed to write to the file.

8. Open `android_winusb.inf` in Notepad.

9. Add these three lines to the `[Google.NTx86]` and `[Google.NTamd64]` sections, and save the file.

   ```
   ;Kindle Fire
   %SingleAdbInterface% = USB_Install, USB\VID_1949&PID_0006
   %CompositeAdbInterface% = USB_Install, USB\VID_1949&PID_0006&MI_01
   ```

10. You will need to set the Kindle to use the Google USB driver that you just edited.

11. In the Windows control panel, **Device Manager**, find the Kindle entry in the list that is under USB.

12. Right-click on the Kindle entry and choose **Update Driver Software...**.

13. Choose the option that lets you find the driver on your local drive, navigate to the `google\usb_driver\` folder, and select it to be the new driver.

14. When the driver is updated, open a command window (handy trick: *Shift*+right-click on the desktop and select **Open command window here**).

15. Change directories to where the ADB tool is located, by typing the following:

```
cd C:\Program Files (x86)\Android\android-sdk\platform-tools\
```

16. Type these three lines, with pressing *Enter* after each line:

```
adb kill-server
adb start-server
adb devices
```

17. You should see the Kindle Fire listed (as an obscure looking number), as well as the virtual device, if you still have that running.

For Mac (MUCH simpler!):

1. Navigate to where the file `adb_usb.ini` is located. On Mac, in **Finder**, select the menu **Go | Go to Folder...**, and type in `~/.android/`.

2. Open the file `adb_usb.ini` in a text editor.

3. On the line after the three instruction lines, type `0x1949`.

4. Make sure there are no blank lines; the last character in the text file would be the `9` at the end of `0x1949`.

5. Save.

6. Open **Utilities | Terminal**.

7. You can let OSX know how to find ADB from anywhere, by typing this line (replace `yourusername` with your user name, and also change the path if you installed the Android SDK to a different location):

```
export PATH=$PATH:/Users/yourusername/Documents/android-sdk-
macosx/platform-tools
```

8. Now, enter the same three lines we did with Windows:

```
adb kill-server
adb start-server
adb devices
```

9. Again, you should see the Kindle Fire listed.

What just happened?

I suspect that you're going to have nightmares about all those steps! It took a lot of searching on the web to find some of those obscure hacks. The general case with Android devices on Windows is that you have to modify the USB driver for the device to be handled by the Google USB driver, and you may have to modify the `adb_usb.ini` file (on Mac too) for the device to be considered as an ADB compatible device.

Getting ready to test for iOS

If you carefully went through all those Android steps, especially on Windows, you will hopefully be amused by the brevity of this section! There is a catch though; you can't really test on an iOS device from LiveCode. We'll look at what you have to do instead in a moment, but first, here are the steps required for testing an app in the iOS simulator.

Time for action – using the iOS simulator

The first steps are much like those for Android apps, but then it gets quicker. Remember, this only applies to Mac OS,and you can only do these things on Windows if you are using Mac OS in a virtual machine, and doing that is most likely not covered by the Mac OS user agreement! In other words, it's best to get a Mac if you intend to develop for iOS.

1. Open LiveCode, create a new **Mainstack**, and save the stack to your hard drive.

2. Select **File | Standalone Application Settings...**.

3. Click on the iOS icon, and select the **Build for iOS** check box.

4. Close the settings dialog box, and take a look at the **Development** menu.

5. You will see a list of simulator options, for iPhone and iPad, and different versions of iOS.

What just happened?

That was it, all it takes to get going with testing using the iOS simulators! Testing on a physical iOS device requires that we create an application first, so let's do that.

Appiness at last!

By this point, you should be able to create a new **Mainstack**, save it, select either iOS or Android in the **Standalone Settings** dialog box, and be able to see simulators or virtual devices in the **Development/Test** menu item. In the case of an Android app, you will also see your device listed, if it is connected via USB at the time.

Time for action – testing a simple stack in the simulators

Feel free to make things that are more elaborate than asked for in these steps! The instructions will be making the assumption that you know how to find things for yourself in the object inspector palette.

1. Open LiveCode, create a new **Mainstack**, and save it to a location where it's easy to find in a moment from now.

2. Set the card window to a size of 1024x768, and uncheck the **Resizable** checkbox.

3. Drag a **label** field into the top-left corner of the card window, and set its contents to something appropriate. Hello World could do nicely!

4. If you're developing on Windows, skip to *step 11*.

5. Open the **Standalone Application** Settings dialog, click on the iOS icon, and select the **Build for iOS** checkbox.

6. Under **Orientation Options**, set the **iPhone initial orientation** to **Landscape**.

7. Close the dialog box.

8. From the **Development/Test Target** sub-menu, choose the **iPad Simulator**.

9. Select **Test** from the **Development** menu.

10. You should be now seeing your test stack running in the iOS simulator!

11. As discussed earlier, launch the Android virtual device.

12. Open the **Standalone Application Settings** dialog box , click on the Android icon, and select the **Build for Android** checkbox.

13. Under **User Interface Options**, set the **initial orientation** to **Landscape**.

14. Close the dialog box.

15. If the virtual device is running by now, do whatever is necessary to get past the locked home screen, if that's what is showing.

16. From the **Development/Test** Target sub-menu, choose the **Android emulator**.

17. Select **Test** from the **Development** menu.

18. You should be now seeing your test stack running in the Android emulator!

What just happened?

All being well, you just made and ran your first mobile app, on both Android and iOS! For an encore, we should try it on physical devices, if only to give Android a chance to show how easy it can be to do that. There is a whole can of worms we haven't yet opened to do with getting an iOS device configured so that it can be used for testing. That is covered in depth in a later chapter, which you could read now, or you could visit the iOS Provisioning Portal at `https://developer.apple.com/ios/manage/overview/index.action`, and look at the *How To* tab in each of the different sections.

Time for action – testing a simple stack on devices

Get your USB cables ready, and connect the devices to your computer. Android first...

1. You should still have **Android** selected in **Standalone Application Settings**.

2. Get your device to its home screen, past the initial lock screen if there is one.

3. Choose **Development/Test Target**, and select your Android device. It may well say `Android` and a very long number.

4. Choose **Development/Test**.

5. The stack should now be running on your Android device.

Now iOS...

1. If you have not read the later chapter on deploying to your device, or the Apple pages, or have not installed certificates and provisioning files, then you will have to skip this test for now.

2. Change the **Standalone Application Settings** back to **iOS**.

3. Under **Basic Application Settings** of the iOS settings is a **Profile** drop-down menu showing the provisioning files that you have installed. Choose the one that is configured for the device you are going to test.

4. Close the dialog box, and choose **Save as Standalone Application...** from the **File** menu.

5. In **Finder**, locate the folder that was just created, and open it to reveal the app file itself. As we didn't give the stack a sensible name, it will be named `Untitled 1`.

6. Open Xcode, which is in the **Developer** folder you created earlier, in the **Applications** sub-folder.

7. In Xcode, choose **Organizer** from the **Window** menu, and select **Devices**, if it isn't already selected.

8. You should see your device listed. Select it, and if you see a button labeled **Use for Development**, click on that button.

9. Drag the app file straight from **Finder** to your device in the **Organizer** window.

10. The small colored circle will turn orange for a moment, and then back to green.

11. You can now open the app on your iOS device!

What just happened?

In addition to getting a test stack working on real devices, we also saw how easy it is, once it's all configured, to test a stack straight to an Android device. If you are developing an app that is to be deployed on both Android and iOS, you may find that the fastest way to work is to test with the iOS Simulator for iOS tests, but to test directly on an Android device instead of using the Android SDK virtual devices.

Have a go hero – Nook

Until recently, the Android support for the Nook Color from Barnes and Noble wasn't good enough for LiveCode apps to be installed. It seems to have improved though, and could well be another worthwhile app store for you to target.

Investigate the signing up process, download their SDK, and so on. With any luck some of what you learned in signing up for the other stores will also apply to the Nook store. Here is your starting point:

```
https://nookdeveloper.barnesandnoble.com
```

Further reading

The SDK providers, Google and Apple, have extensive pages of information on setting up their development environments, creating certificates and provisioning files, and so on. The information does have to cover a lot of topics that don't apply to LiveCode, so try not to get lost! These would be good starting pages:

- `http://developer.android.com/`
- `http://developer.apple.com/ios/`

Summary

Signing up for programs, file downloading, command-lining your way all over the place, and patiently waiting for the Android emulator to launch, means that it could take the best part of a day to work through what we've covered in this chapter! Fortunately, you only have to go through it once.

We did work through the tasks that you have to do before you can create a mobile app in LiveCode:

♦ Download and install the Android SDK

♦ Sign up as an iOS developer

♦ Download and install Xcode and the iOS SDKs

♦ Configure devices and simulators

We also covered some topics that will be useful once you are ready to upload a finished app:

♦ Signing up for Android Market

♦ Signing up for Amazon Appstore

There will be more mundane things to cover near the end of the book, but not for a while! Next up, we will start to play with some of the special abilities of mobile devices.

3

Building User Interfaces

So many different screens!

When making utility or game applications for desktop computers you can often get away with having a particular sized window, for which you can make custom graphics that fit exactly. With mobile devices you have to cope with a wide range of screen sizes, and aspect ratios, and also have interface elements that look correct for the operating system on the user's device.

LiveCode is capable of publishing on Mac, Windows, and Linux, and goes some way towards solving the difficulty of making interface elements look right for each platform. The **View** menu has a **Look and Feel** menu item where you can choose between **Native Theme**, **Mac OS Classic**, **Windows 95**, and **Motif**. The same isn't true for mobile operating systems; all controls look like **Motif**. You still have two choices; you can create graphics that look like they belong in your target OS, or you can call native routines in order to have the system itself present the correct looking controls.

In this chapter we will:

- ◆ Set up a "test bed" mobile application
- ◆ Open e-mail and browser windows
- ◆ Show a date picker control
- ◆ Load pictures from the library and camera
- ◆ Make an iOS looking button
- ◆ Manually lay out an interface
- ◆ Use code to lay out an interface
- ◆ Look at a powerful mobile interface controls add-on

Setting up a test bed mobile app

As a proving ground for the things we're going to try, we'll set up a single mobile app that has multiple screens, one for each of the things we want to test.

What to call the test bed app?

We could call it almost anything, but we'll let the iPhone help make the decision for us. On the iPhone, and iPod touch, there is only a small amount of space under the home screen icons for the name to appear. iOS will take your nice long app name and will show a shortened version of the name, using ellipses to concatenate the ends of the name together. "My super duper app" will appear as "My sup...app" - not quite as informative! The number of letters that can appear without it being truncated will vary depending on the width of the letters used, but typically it is a limit of 11 letters. So, we will call the test bed app "LC Test Bed", which is exactly 11 letters!

Time for action – making the test bed stack

Before we create the iOS and Android apps, we should get what we want going as a LiveCode stack, and fully test it on our desktop computers. These steps are going to assume you know how to do what is asked in LiveCode, without precise instructions.

1. Open LiveCode, create a new **Mainstack**, and **Save** it as `LCTestBed`.

2. Set the size to `320x480`. Just to make sure that the things will appear on the smallest of screens. The things we make will be in the upper left-hand side area of larger screens.

3. We're going to make a button for each card in the stack. Start by making one named `Menu`.

4. Name the first card `Menu`.

5. Add buttons for **Email**, **Browser**, **DatePicker**, and **Picture**. Make sure the buttons are big enough to touch on your devices. You should have something like the following screenshot:

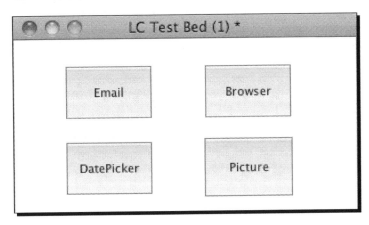

6. Create four new cards. Name each one such that it matches with one of the button names.

7. Coming back to the first card, set the script of each button such that it goes to the matching card, with this script:

```
on mouseUp
    go card the short name of me
end mouseUp
```

8. On each card, create a button to return to the menu card. Name the button `Menu`. Set its script to the same as the other buttons.

9. Select the **Run** (browse) tool, and try clicking the buttons, to jump to each of the four cards and back to the menu card.

What just happened?

Well, nothing too exciting! But you should now have five cards and the ability to move between the menu card and the others. Now we're going to add scripts to each card to help illustrate the various features. The most efficient approach would be to add all of the scripts and related buttons and fields, and then test the final test bed app in one go. But where's the fun in that? Therefore, we'll create one feature at a time.

Invoking the desktop e-mail application

There are many cases where you may want to hear from the users of your applications. Perhaps you want them to e-mail suggested improvements, or to let them ask you questions. You could easily launch their e-mail program, and then leave them to figure out what to write. Alternatively, you could automatically set the "To" address, the subject, and even some of the body of the message. At the very least it could make your life easier, because you could filter incoming e-mails based on something that you placed into the subject field.

Time for action – calling the native e-mail application

We'll make some fields and a button to try out sending an e-mail feature.

1. Go to the e-mail card and create four fields. Name them `From`, `CC`, `Subject`, and `Body`.

2. Make a button named `Test`.

3. In the **Test** button, type the following script:

```
on mouseUp
    put field "To" into toText
    put field "CC" into ccText
    put field "Subject" into subjectText
    put field "Body" into bodyText
    revMail toText,ccText,subjectText,bodyText
end mouseup
```

4. Select the **Run** tool and type example information into each of the fields.

5. Click on the **Test** button.

What just happened?

One neat thing about LiveCode syntax is that the code for mobile applications also works for desktop applications, and vice versa. All being well, when you clicked the **Test** button you found yourself in your default e-mail application, ready to send the message that you had entered in the LiveCode stack fields.

Installing the e-mail test onto devices

It's no great surprise that the desktop test worked; the ability to open other applications is a basic feature of LiveCode. Still, it's neat to be able to set some initial text for the new message to use. Next we should see if this can work on devices as well.

Time for action – trying test bed stack on devices

Connect your Android and/or iOS device to your computer using USB. These instructions are almost the same as those in the previous chapter, where we tested a Hello World stack, and after this point any directions will be briefer, based on the assumption that you know the steps needed to test an app on your device. Chapter 7, *Deploying to Your Device*, describes all of the options in the **Standalone Applications Settings** dialog box, but for the moment we're only going to fill in a few details, so here we will view just a portion of the dialog, starting with the Android settings.

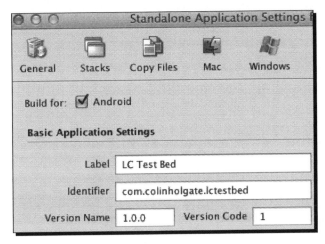

1. Make sure that **Android** is checked in the **Standalone Application Settings** dialog box.

2. In the **Identifier** field, type in an identifier that will be unique. com.yourname. lctestbed would do.

3. Get your device to its home screen, past the initial lock screen if there is one.

4. In LiveCode, choose **Development/Test Target**, and select your Android device. It will be named Android followed by a long number.

5. Choose **Development/Test**.

6. After being compiled, the stack should run on your Android device, and you should be able to touch the **Email** button and create a test message that will use the Android e-mail application.

7. Moving on to iOS, if you haven't done so, read Chapter 7, *Deploying to Your Device*, or read at least those parts that show how to install your iOS developer certificates and provisioning files. As with Android, we're only going to change a couple of items in the **Standalone Application Settings** dialog box. Here is the area that we'll be changing:

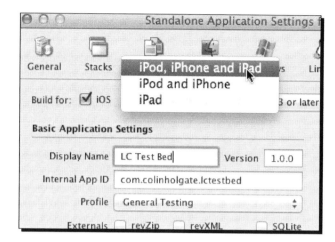

8. Change the **Standalone Application Settings** to **iOS**.

9. Under the **Basic Application Settings** section of the iOS settings is a **Profile** drop-down menu of the provisioning files that you have installed. Choose one that is configured for the device you are going to test on.

10. In the **Internal App ID** field type in a unique ID. As with Android, com.yourname.lctestbed would do. yourname would of course be your name, or your company name.

11. If you are testing on iPad, select the **iPod, iPhone and iPad** option from the **Supported Devices** drop-down menu.

12. Close the dialog box, and choose **Save as Standalone Application...** from the **File** menu.

13. When the save is completed you may see a warning message, telling you about missing splash screens and icons. Ignore these for now.

14. In **Finder**, locate the folder that was just created, and open it to reveal the app file itself.

15. Open **Xcode** and choose **Organizer** from the **Window** menu, and then select **Devices**, if it isn't already selected.

16. You should see your device listed. Select it, and if you see a button labeled **Use for Development**, click on that button.

17. Drag the app file straight from the **Finder** window to your device in the **Organizer** window.

18. The small colored circle next to the device will turn orange for a moment, and then back to green.

19. You can now open the app and try the **Email** button to create a test message, which will use the standard iOS Mail application.

What just happened?

We have gone through the steps needed to install the test bed app onto both Android and iOS devices. We also had to change a couple of things in the **Standalone Application Settings** dialog box. As you saw, there are quite a lot of settings there. You can look forward to learning about them all in Chapter 7, *Deploying to Your Device*

Opening a web page

Another need in your application is to be able to present additional online information. You want the user to click on a link, or touch as the case may be, and be taken to a page that lists all of the other applications they can buy from you!

Time for action – calling the native browser application

This next test will go faster. Or at least the instructions will be briefer, as we will condense some of the steps into more concise directions.

1. Copy the **Test** button on the **Email** card, and paste it onto the **Browser** card, just to save you some time making the button look nice.

2. Edit the **Test** button script, and change it to the following:

```
on mouseUp
    launch url "http://www.runrev.com/"
end mouseUp
```

3. Choose the **Run** tool and click on the **Test** button. You should see the RunRev home page in your default browser.

Trying the app on devices is exactly the same as with testing the e-mail feature. For Android:

1. Select Android in the **Standalone Application Settings** dialog box.

2. Select your Android device as the test target from the **Development** menu (most likely it will already be selected from your previous test).

3. Select **Test** from the **Development** menu.

4. The previous test of the app will be overwritten, and the new version launched automatically.

5. Try the **Browser** button, and then the **Test** button that you just created on the Browser card. The runrev.com page should be opened.

For iOS:

1. Select iOS in the Standalone Application Settings dialog box.

2. Redo the **Save as Standalone Application**, drag the app file onto your device in the Organizer window of Xcode, as you did the first time.

3. Try the **Browser** and **Test** buttons; you should see the RunRev home page opened inside Safari.

What just happened?

As with the E-mail test, adding the standard code for opening a web page works for Android and iOS, just as it does for a desktop computer.

If you are testing on both Android and iOS, you will notice that the behavior is different when you return from looking at a web page. With Android you can press the back arrow button and still be on the Browser card of your stack. With iOS the stack is restarted when you return. One solution to this that we will examine later is to write data to an external file, so that when the app is reopened we can return the user to where they were before leaving the app.

Mobile-only, date picker

The next couple of examples we will try are the ones that only work on mobile devices, not on desktop computers.

Time for action – showing a date picker

Many applications will require the user to choose a date for an event, and with mobile devices there is a particular look to the "date picker" that you are shown. LiveCode lets us display such a control.

1. Copy the **Test** button from the **Browser** card, and paste it onto the **DatePicker** card.

2. Change the script to the following:

```
on mouseUp
    iphonePickDate "date"
end mouseUp
```

3. Select the Run tool and try the **Test** button. You'll see an error, because this is a mobile-only feature.

4. For a change, select **iPhone** or **iPad Simulator** from the **Development/Test Target** menu, and then choose **Test** from the **Development** menu.

5. You will see your stack open in the iOS simulator, and you can try the **DatePicker** and **Test** buttons, to see the iOS date picker being displayed.

6. Perform the same old **Save As** and install using the **Organizer** window steps in order to try the date picker on your iOS device.

7. Touch the **DatePicker** button on the menu card, and the **Test** button on the datepicker card. An iOS native date picker should appear.

What just happened?

Hopefully you're getting faster at building and installing mobile apps by now! In addition to testing again on a device, we also tried out the simulator. Generally speaking it is fastest to test what you can with the iOS simulator, and only test on a device when you're checking things like multi-touch, accelerometer, and camera support.

Mobile-only, loading pictures

Maybe one day it will be possible to bring in images from the user's desktop computer photo application, or from their web camera, but for now these are features that only work on mobile devices.

Time for action – loading pictures

LiveCode can call upon the native photo library and camera apps. We will test both of these on Android and iOS, but of course only if your device has some saved images, and a camera. For the Kindle Fire, which doesn't have a camera, make sure to save some pictures into the Gallery app, so that we can at least try loading those.

1. Copy the **Test** button from the **DatePicker** card, and paste it twice onto the **Pictures** card. Change the name of the buttons to `Test Camera` and `Test Library`.

2. Edit the script of the `Test Camera` button to the following:

```
on mouseUp
    mobilePickPhoto "camera"
end mouseup
```

3. Edit the script of the `Test Library` button to the following:

```
on mouseUp
    mobilePickPhoto "library"
end mouseup
```

4. As we test the loading of pictures, the image that is loaded will cover the test buttons, stopping us from returning to the menu card. To solve this issue, add this to the card script:

```
on mouseup
    if word 1 of the target is "image" then delete the target
end mouseup
```

5. Go into **Standalone Application Settings**, and select **Android**.

6. We have to ask Android OS for permission to use the camera, and to store the image, so check the boxes for **Camera** and **Write External Storage** as shown in the following screenshot:

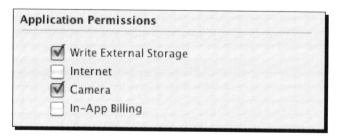

7. Repeat the usual steps for testing on your Android device, or installing on your iOS device.

8. Once the app is running on your device, touch **Pictures** on the first screen, and then **Test Library**. You should see the typical OS-specific options for choosing a picture from your library or gallery.

9. The picture you have selected is loaded onto the card window, and will fill most of the screen, obscuring our **Test** and **Menu** buttons. The card script we entered will mean that you can touch the image to delete it, and then try another test.

10. Try the **Test Camera** button. You will see the OS-specific camera application, and when you have taken a picture and touched the **Use** or **OK** button in the camera application, the image will be placed onto the **Pictures** card.

What just happened?

These simple scripts illustrate how LiveCode is able to call the OS-specific applications to do what would otherwise take a lot of coding. Even better, as later versions of iOS and Android operating systems are released, the same simple scripts will activate the more advanced features that Apple and Google have implemented.

Pop quiz – getting the big picture

We take so much for granted when it comes to improvements in technology. You might feel hard done by if your phone's camera is a measly 2 megapixels, but think back to how things were long ago, and how big a picture you were used to seeing. In terms of the number of pixels, how many original Macintosh screens can fit in the area shown by a single 8-megapixel photo?

a.   4

b.   15

c.   24

d.   45

Making OS styled buttons

It's nice that LiveCode can call upon OS native controls, but that raises a problem because the standard Motif-styled buttons will look ugly by comparison. We can fix that either by using some built-in features of LiveCode, or with the use of an add-on product.

Using bitmaps

As we saw in *Chapter 1, LiveCode Fundamentals*, you can use different bitmaps for the button states. You could get such images by taking screenshots of the buttons on your mobile device at least with iOS and Android OS v4 and later, or you can save a lot of time by downloading files that others have made available. Some of these files are only licensed for use in prototypes, but we'll take a look at one that is also licensed for use in commercial products.

Time for action – using Photoshop to prepare button states

The file we are going to use has Photoshop filter effects that GIMP cannot handle, so unfortunately you will need Photoshop to follow these steps, or at least a friend who has Photoshop!

1. Read the article from the following link:

    ```
    http://spin.atomicobject.com/2011/03/07/photoshop-template-for-
    ios-buttons/
    ```

2. The article points to some other sources of information, but for now just download this file:

    ```
    http://spin.atomicobject.com/assets/2011/3/7/iOS_Buttons.psd
    ```

3. Open the file in Photoshop (it may open automatically).

4. In the **Layers** palette hide the layers named **Background** and **Tool Bar – Retina**.

5. Expand the layer named **Bar Button – Retina**, and hide the **Button Label** layer.

6. Use the **Marquee** tool to select an area around the upper right-hand side button. It should now look like the following:

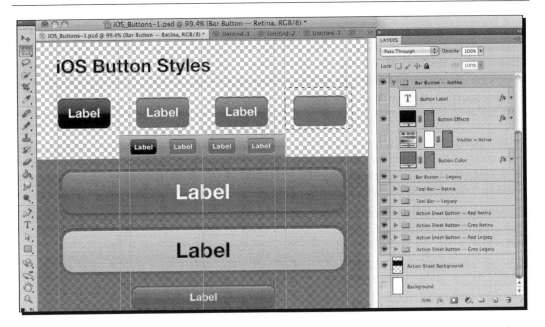

7. Choose **Copy Merged** from the **Edit** menu.

8. Select **New** from the **File** menu, make sure the **Background Contents** are set to **Transparent**, and accept the size you are given.

9. Select **Paste**, it will be an exact fit, and you will see the idle state for that button.

10. Choose **Save for Web & Devices...** from the **File** menu.

11. In the save dialog box select **24 bit PNG**, and make sure the **Transparency** box is checked. Save the PNG file with a suitable name, say `bluebuttonup.png`.

12. Return to the main document and turn on the layer **Visible = Active**.

13. Do another **Copy Merged**, **New**, **Paste**, and **Save for Web & Devices...**.

14. Save the PNG as `bluebuttondown.png`.

15. Go back into LiveCode.

16. Reopen the test bed stack.

17. Use **File | Import As Control | Image File...** to bring the two PNG files into the stack.

18. You can place the two images anywhere. Uncheck **Visible** in **Basic Properties** for each image.

19. Add a new button to the first card, and give it the name `Location`.

20. Set the button script to:

```
on mouseUp
   iphoneStartTrackingLocation
   put iphoneCurrentLocation() into theLocation
   answer theLocation["latitude"]
end mouseUp
```

21. Select the `Location` button, and in **Basic Properties** of the **Inspector** palette, turn off **Show name** and **Opaque**.

22. In **Icons & Border**, turn off **Three D**, **Border**, and **Hilite border**.

23. Click on the magic wand button next to the **Icon** entry in the **Inspector** palette.

24. From the **Image library** drop-down menu, select **This Stack**.

25. Click on the lighter of the two blue images.

26. Click the magic wand button next to the **Hilite icon** entry, and then click on the darker of the two images.

27. Resize the button to be just big enough to show the blue image without it being cropped.

28. Place a **Label** field on top of the button.

29. In **Basic Properties**, check the **Disabled** box. This is to make sure the field doesn't trap the click you are going to do. We want the button to get that click.

30. In **Contents**, enter `Location`.

31. Under **Text Formatting**, set the field to use `Helvetica Neue`, `18` point, `Bold`, and `center` aligned.

32. Under **Colors & Palettes**, set the text color to be white.

33. Align the field and the button so that the two are centered on each other.

34. If you now test using the iOS simulator and click on the `Location` button, you will just see a zero, but testing on a device should display your latitude when you touch the button (you will have to give permission for the app to know your location the first time you press the button).

What just happened?

Although the button we made may not be the perfect size, or even have the correct look for a standalone iOS button, we did go through all of the steps that you would need to make button state images. Placing a LiveCode field over the image buttons doesn't necessarily give the best appearance. In reality, you would take more time in Photoshop to make the right width button for the label you're using, and might also add the text to the image itself. It would look better, and you will not need to use a field to show the button's name in LiveCode.

LiveCode is able to use code to create the images we need, by setting the points of a graphic, and also its `fillGradient`. But once you have the component parts needed to simulate a button or other kind of control, it will still take a lot more scripting to manage those elements.

There is an easy way out though, but it will cost you $50!

Pop quiz – the cost of things these days

As with the increase in your expectations for the size of a digital photo, you also expect to get a lot more for your money these days. While you weigh up the advantages of spending $50, how much better value do you think a computer memory is now compared to 25 years ago?

- a. 10 times better
- b. Half as good
- c. 100 times better
- d. 6,000 times better!

MobGUI to the rescue!

RunRev is based in Edinburgh, Scotland, and they are a talented bunch! But they are not the only talented Scottish folk, there is also John Craig. He has developed a powerful add-on to LiveCode that includes an increasingly long list of iOS and Android OS looking controls. If you were to buy his product you would pay $50, for which you get the current version plus any updates that are released in the 12 months following your purchase date. While taking a look at it here, we can use a trial version of the product.

Time for action – getting started with MobGUI

As with other add-ons to LiveCode, MobGUI will need to be installed into the LiveCode plugins folder. On Windows that will be `My Documents/My LiveCode/Plugins`. On Mac it will be `~/Documents/My LiveCode/Plugins`.

1. Download the latest version of MobGUI from `http://mobgui.com/download.php`.

2. The zip file will expand to become a LiveCode stack, named `revMobGUI.livecode`.

3. Drag the stack into the `plugins` folder, and reopen LiveCode.

4. Make a new `Maintstack`.

5. From the **Development** menu, choose **Plugins/revMobGUI**. This window will appear:

6. The first of the icons is the splash screen, and the last five icons are for things such as registering, support, and getting updates. Click on the second icon, the one that looks like a play button. You will see this arrangement:

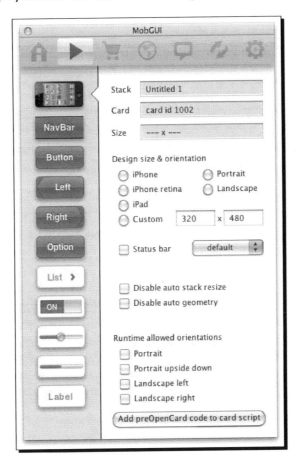

7. The **MobGUI** window is much like a combination of the LiveCode **Tool** and **Inspector** palettes.

8. Try dragging different items onto the card, and look at the options for each item.

9. Right-click on the iPhone image, to see that you can switch between different sets of controls.

10. Select the **iOS Controls 2** from the list you see.

11. Drag a **TabBar** onto the **card** window; note how it snaps to the bottom.

12. Right-click on the **Button** control, and select **4** from the list.

13. You'll see that you can now drag and create four buttons in one go.

14. *Alt*+double-click on one of the new buttons you just made. The buttons will spread out to fill the width of the card.

What just happened?

One remarkable thing about LiveCode is that the many windows and palettes you use in the program are all just stacks, and we've started to make use of a specialized stack that is going to save us a lot of time, and will give us a nice OS-specific looking interface.

Test bed app, the MobGUI way

We're going to make much the same test bed app, but in this we'll try to give a more iOS look to the app.

Time for action – using MobGUI to make a test bed app

As you work in LiveCode and start new stacks, save and close other previously opened stacks, as they can still be occupying memory. Sometimes you can get into a confused state where you're making a new untitled stack, only to find that there's already an untitled stack on the go, which you're asked if you want to purge. So why not treat yourself to a quit and fresh launch of LiveCode!

1. Create a new **Mainstack**. Set the name to MGTestBed, and save it somewhere you can easily find. Perhaps in the folder with the LCTestBed stack, which was feeling lonely!

2. Open the **MobGUI** window, by selecting **Development/Plugins/revMobGUI**.

3. In the **MobGUI** window's page of controls you will see that you can choose a size for the stack. Choose the **iPhone** size, and the stack will become 320x480.

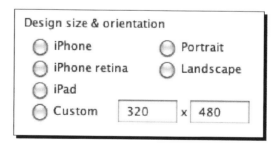

4. Click on the button named **Add preOpenCard code to card script**. This will insert the code needed to initialize **MobGUI**.

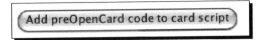

5. Set the name of this first card to Email.

6. Remember that you can switch between the different sets of controls by right-clicking on the image of the iPhone. From that menu, select **iOS Controls 2**.

7. Drag the **BG** control onto the card. It will create a background layer.

8. Drag a tab bar onto the card window. It will snap to the bottom of the card window, and also resize to the width of the card.

9. Right-click on the button control in the **MobGUI** window, and select **4**.

10. Drag the buttons onto the card window, on top of the tab bar. Four buttons will be added.

11. Most likely the buttons will be off to the right-hand side of where they should be. *Alt*+double-click on one of the buttons, to resize and spread it across the width of the card window. If need be, select the buttons and nudge them up or down to make them sit nicely against the TabBar.

12. Select each button and set the names and labels to Email, Browser, DatePicker, and Picture.

13. Select the Email button and choose **Object Script** from the **Object** menu, or right-click on the button and choose the **Edit Script** option. The script will look like this:

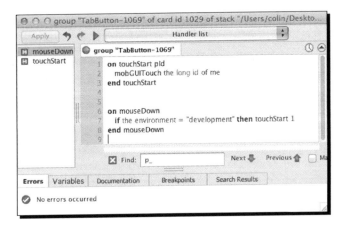

14. You can add to the script. Modify the `touchStart` handler so that it looks like the following:

```
on touchStart pId
   mobGUITouch the long id of me
go card the short name of me
end touchStart
```

15. You can copy the whole script from the first button, and paste it into the other three buttons.

16. We'll need these elements on all of the four cards we're going to make, so select all and then choose **Group Selected** from the **Object** menu.

17. Make sure the group is selected, and in the regular LiveCode **Inspector** palette, check the **Behave like a background** box.

18. Make three more cards, and name them `Browser`, `DatePicker`, and `Picture`.

19. From the menu where you chose **iOS Controls 2**, choose **iOS Controls 1**.

20. Drag the NavBar control onto the card window for each of the four cards, and set the name to match the card's name,

21. In **Standalone Application Settings**, choose either iOS or Android, depending on the device you want to test on.

22. Set the **Internal App ID**, or **Identifier**, to `com.yourname.MGTestBed`.

23. If you're using iOS, make sure to choose a profile from the Profile drop-down menu.

24. You can now do a **Test** from the **Development** menu, having first chosen either iPhone Simulator, or your connected Android device.

What just happened?

It seems like quite a few steps, but shouldn't take too much time, and we already have the navigation between the four cards looking like an authentic iOS interface.

Now let's get some of the test features going, but in a more native, integrated way than before.

MobGUI native controls

One powerful feature of **MobGUI** is that it can use ordinary LiveCode controls as placeholders for what will become native controls when you run the app on a device. This is something that you can do for yourself with code, but being able to move placeholder controls around until you like the layout will save a lot of time.

Time for action – using native controls from MobGUI

Right-click on the little image of the iPhone in the **MobGUI** window, and make sure that you're on the Native iOS Controls set.

1. Go to the **Email** card and drag three Text controls and one Multiline Text control from the Native iOS Controls set in the **MobGUI** window.

2. Name the Text controls as To, CC, and Subject, and the Multiline Text control as Body. The size of the Body should be made big enough to enter a few lines of text.

3. As you create each field, note that you can set the keyboard type. Set it to Email for the To and CC fields.

4. From iOS Controls 1 set and drag two Buttons onto the card window. Name one Done, and the other Send. You should have something that looks like the following screenshot:

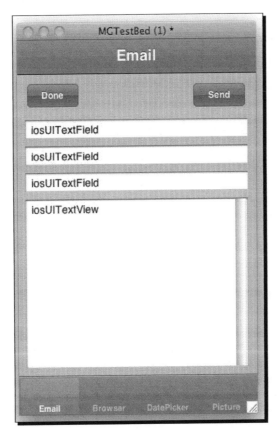

5. When we test the app and touch one of the fields, the keyboard overlay will appear. We'll use the `Done` button as a way to hide the keyboard. Add a focus line to the `touchEnd` handler of the `Done` button script:

```
on touchEnd pId
    mobGUIUntouch the long id of me
    focus on nothing
        --other lines
end touchEnd
```

6. **MobGUI** can retrieve properties from these native fields, using a `mobFieldGet` function. Change the **Send** button's `touchEnd` handler to use that function for each field, and to also call the `revMail` function:

```
on touchEnd pId
    mobGUIUntouch the long id of me
    put mobFieldGet("To", "text") into totext
    put mobFieldGet("CC", "text") into cctext
    put mobFieldGet("Subject", "text") into subjecttext
    put mobFieldGet("Body", "text") into bodytext
    revMail totext,cctext,subjecttext,bodytext
end touchEnd
```

7. Go to the Browser card.

8. From the Native iOS Controls set, drag a Text control to the card window, and name it `URL`.

9. Drag a browser control (the one that shows Google as its image) to the card window, and name it `Page`.

10. Adjust the sizes so that the text field fills the width of the card, and the browser control fills the area between the text field and the tab bar at the bottom.

11. Select the browser control, and in the MobGUI window enter a value for URL. This will make the browser control load that URL as its first page.

12. Edit the script of the URL text field, and add this handler:

```
on inputReturnKey
    mobBrowserSet "Page","url",mobFieldGet("URL","text")
end inputReturnKey
```

13. Try another Test, and go to the Email and Browser cards to see them in action.

What just happened?

We recreated the first two tests from our earlier test bed app, but now it looks a lot nicer! We also made use of MobGUI's ability to get and set data in native iOS controls, in this case by using `mobFieldGet` and `mobBrowserSet`.

Have a go hero – other tests and pretty icons

Go ahead and add the other two tests to the stack.

For the `DatePicker` example, add an `OpenCard` handler to the card that includes the line: `iphonePickDate date`.

For the Picture test, look at the four steps in the *Time for action – loading pictures* section earlier in this chapter. However this time you will be adding the lines to native buttons, and inserting the lines into the `touchEnd` handler instead of a `mouseUp` handler.

For a bonus, edit the tab bar group and select one of the buttons. In the **MobGUI** window you will see that you can set custom icons for the **Dim** and **Active** states for each button. If you perform a Google image search for `free mobile icons`, you should be able to find lots of examples that would look nice on the four buttons we made.

Adjusting things for different screen sizes

So far we have only tested using an iPhone size, and only the Portrait orientation. You may well want to use the same stack for iPhone and iPad, or perhaps iPad and an Android tablet, which have quite different aspect ratios.

Even if you stick only to the iPhone, you would still want to take care of Portrait and Landscape orientations. We therefore have to find ways to arrange the many controls on the card to look their best for each screen size and orientation.

There are several ways to achieve this. Firstly we'll look at using a resize handler.

Layout using a resize handler

When a stack's window size changes, LiveCode sends a `resizeStack` message that we can trap, in order to rearrange the controls for the new width and height.

Time for action – simple code layout example

It could get quite complicated if you laid out all of the card's controls with code, so we're only going to construct a simple case, to show the technique. You can enhance this later for more complex cases.

1. Create a new **Mainstack**.

2. Add four buttons across the width of the card.

3. Put this handler into the card script:

```
on resizeStack newWidth,newHeight
    put the width of button 1 into buttonWidth
    put (newWidth - 4 * buttonWidth)/5 into gap
    put the top of button 1 into buttonTop
    repeat with a = 1 to 4
        set the top of button a to buttonTop
        set the left of button a to gap + (a-1) * (gap+buttonWidth)
    end repeat
    pass resizeStack
end resizeStack
```

4. Resize the card window. The buttons should spread out evenly across the card.

5. Go to **Standalone Application Settings** and select the **iOS** option.

6. Make sure that the supported devices include iPad.

7. Set the orientation options to include all four orientations.

8. From the **Development** menu set the **Test Target** to be the **iPad Simulator**, and do a Test.

9. In the simulator, choose either **Rotate Left** or **Rotate Right**, from the **Hardware** menu.

10. The buttons should spread themselves out across the screen in both portrait and landscape orientations.

What just happened?

In addition to making a simple example of how the `resizeStack` handler can be used, we also saw that orientation changes send the `resizeStack` message.

Layout using the LiveCode Geometry Manager

While a control is selected on the card, the **Inspector** palette has an entry named **Geometry**. It's a somewhat strange interface! Let's take a look.

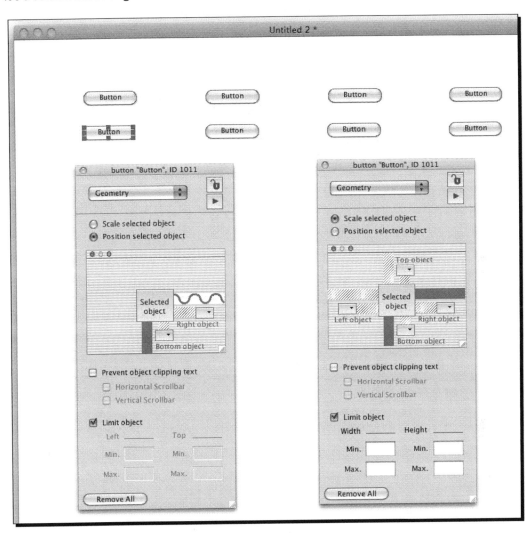

Those faint horizontal and vertical bars are used to select whether you want the control to be scaled or positioned by a fixed or relative amount. That is, if a button is 100 pixels from the right-hand side of the card window, and you select the position to be a fixed distance away, as you resize the card window the button will remain 100 pixels from the right-hand side edge of the window. If, on the other hand, you use the relative setting, and the button is 80 percent across the card window, it will still be 80 percent across the window after you have resized it.

The first click on one of those bars will make it turn solid red in color, which indicates that it's a fixed distance from the edge of the card. If you click again it becomes a red waveform, indicating that it's going to be relative.

In the previous screenshot you can see that the selected button is set to be a fixed distance from the bottom of the card, and a relative distance from the right-hand side of the card. The image also shows the scaling settings for the control.

Time for action – using the Geometry Manager to position buttons

Now we'll add some buttons to the stack we have going. One thing to know: the layout features in MobGUI (that we will look at next) are in competition with the Geometry Manager, so if you still have that open from earlier, click on the check box that says "**Disable auto geometry**.

1. Take the first four buttons and duplicate them, to give another set of four below the first ones.

2. Select the first of the new buttons and in the **Geometry** section of the **Inspector** palette click once on the vertical bar, and twice on the horizontal bar, ending with the state shown in the screenshot.

3. Do the same for the other three buttons.

4. Try resizing the card window.

What just happened?

That was quite a quick test, and if all went well you will see that resizing the card window is positioning the first four buttons using the `resizeStack` handler we added, and positioning the second set of four buttons using the Geometry Manager. With the settings we used, the results should be much the same, except that the second set of four buttons will remain a fixed distance away from the bottom of the card window.

There is a lot of power in the Geometry Manager, and you should take a look at the other abilities it has from the reference link shown at the end of this chapter. But it happens not to be the best way to deal with mobile screen sizes. Yet again, **MobGUI** to the rescue!

Layout using MobGUI

The layout approach used by the Geometry Manager is geared towards desktop applications, where the user is quite likely to resize the window to an unknown amount. With mobile apps, the layout only changes once as the app loads, and then each time the orientation changes. When it does change it will be changing between only two different sizes. It's a much simpler situation than resizing a desktop application's window to an arbitrary size.

MobGUI uses a different approach to solving the general problem, which has advantages when it comes to mobile apps.

Time for action – using MobGUI to remember layouts for us

If you were following along there, and checked the **MobGUI** window box to disable auto geometry, uncheck it again. We're going to need it!

1. Create a new **Mainstack**.

2. Using the **MobGUI** window, set the card window to be iPhone sized and Landscape.

3. Drag a NavBar control onto the card.

4. Drag a TabBar onto the card.

5. Right-click on the **MobGUI** button control, and select 4, then drag those four buttons onto the TabBar you just added.

6. *Alt*+double-click on one of those buttons to spread them out, and also move them vertically to be nicely positioned against the TabBar.

7. Click on the iPhone picture in the **MobGUI** window, and change the orientation to be Portrait.

8. Select the TabBar and its buttons, and move them to the bottom of the portrait card window.

9. Use the *Alt*+double-click trick to make the TabBar, the NavBar, and the buttons, spread themselves across the width of the portrait card window.

10. Try clicking on the Portrait and Landscape buttons. The layout should change to what you had carefully created.

What just happened?

This approach of MobGUI's, where it remembers the layout for each of the possible screen sizes and orientations, just seems to make more sense for mobile usage. The Geometry Manager is certainly more powerful and flexible, but in reality you want to carefully layout the different arrangements to be the best possible for a given sized screen, rather than relying on arithmetic to reposition everything for you.

Have a go hero – other sizes

We just made the card lay itself out nicely for iPhone portrait and landscape modes. Now do the same again, for iPad portrait and landscape modes, and also for a custom screen size of 800x480, in both portrait and landscape.

 One time saving tip is that you can select all of the controls before doing the *Alt*+double-click. It will make the NavBar, TabBar, and buttons, spread out all in one go.

Further reading

As mentioned above, the Geometry Manager has a lot of powerful features. We're going to be sticking with the MobGUI approach, but if you're also interested in desktop applications, take a look at the lesson at this page:

`http://lessons.runrev.com/s/lessons/m/4067/l/19026-Geometry-Manager`

Summary

The trick with easy to use tools, such as LiveCode, is to create mobile apps that users will think were created with the harder to use native tools, such as Xcode. You can achieve that because of LiveCode's ability to call upon native features, and because you can make interfaces that look correct.

In this chapter we covered several ways to achieve that goal:

◆ Calling native OS features, using simple LiveCode commands

◆ Preparing images to be used for button states

◆ Making OS-specific looking buttons by adding those images

◆ Creating iOS native looking controls with **MobGUI**

◆ Laying out the interface with code, the Geometry Manager, and MobGUI

So far these have all been small test stacks, to get us warmed up! Next up we're going to look at general application structure, and make a fully-fledged utility application.

4

Using Remote Data and Media

Data needs to get out more!

Applications can be made where all of the supporting data is within the application, but quite often we want to show data that is out in the real world somewhere, and also to save information (a high score list perhaps) to files that are external to the application.

When creating a LiveCode application we need to think about the structure of the stack, its code, and the data it uses.

In this chapter we will:

◆ Look at the various ways a stack might be structured

◆ Think about where code should go

◆ Write to and read from external text files

◆ Create a scrapbook-like app for remembering interesting Internet based media files

Don't forget to download the sample files!

There are a lot of lines of code in this chapter. The code is shown along with explanations about each function, and you could build up something that matched the corresponding sample file. But it would be very easy to make a mistake while transcribing the scripts, both in terms of what the script says, and where the script should be placed. It may be safer to study the sample files and to read the overall description here. You can download the code from the Packt site.

Stack structure

There are two aspects to how a stack may be structured. One is to do with how user interface elements are organized, and the other is about where in the hierarchy of a stack you should place your code.

Code driven and manually created layouts

If you imagine how a typical mobile application appears, it could be something along these lines:

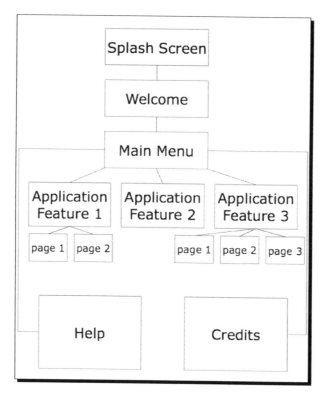

Sometimes applications are entirely code driven, where every screen you see is created using code at the time that it's needed. Or perhaps it would be already laid out elements that are saved as resources, and then the code loads those resources. In either case the whole application could take place on the equivalent of one LiveCode card.

Another approach would be to lay out every possible screen combination as different cards, or even stacks, and go to the card or stack that looks like the app should at that moment.

In the first case you would need to run the application and go through the user actions in order to see if the layout was correct, then go back and change code or resources, and try again. In the second case you may be faced with a lot of layout combinations.

As we start to make apps here, we'll try to find a middle ground, where we'll use cards to set up the main screens we'll need, and then use code to show and hide other elements. The goal is to try and be efficient, and not create complex code for laying out items that could be done quickly by hand, or to use lots of images when a small amount of code could get the same results.

Locations for code

LiveCode is extremely flexible in terms of how you structure the things you make with it. In addition to a dozen different kinds of control that could contain code, you can have front scripts, groups, the current card, a mainstack, stacks in use, back script, and LiveCode itself. This diagram shows only a few example controls, but gives you the sense of how many levels there are to the hierarchy in LiveCode:

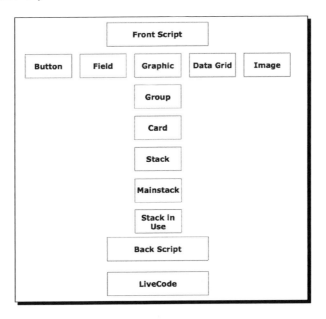

You can also have sub stacks, which are often used to show dialog windows, the ability to add front and back scripts, and you can put stacks into and out of use. Overall it can get quite confusing!

It is largely a case of personal style as to where you put your scripts, and often you may have a reasonable argument as to why you did it a certain way. You could argue that all of the action that is to take place should be in the script of the button that you clicked on. It would make it easy to edit all of the handlers involved, and if you needed the same features in another stack you would only have to copy the button across. However, if you had a number of those buttons on the screen, and needed to make changes, you would have to do so to all of them.

Another valid argument would be to say that all handlers would be at the stack level. You would then have one central place to make changes, but you would have to do lots of "if statements" to check which control had been operated on.

You might want to reuse routines that you have developed over time, and would have a set of stacks that you put into use, each stack handling only a particular aspect of the task at hand. In the world of **Object Oriented Programming (OOP)** it's quite common to extend this approach to a crazy degree, with hundreds, or even thousands, of small files that each handle a tiny portion of the overall application.

We won't go to any of these extremes. Instead we will try to put code at the lowest level that it needs to be without having to duplicate the code as you make additional controls that need that same code. To do that we will try to think ahead and try to spot efficiencies that we can use. Let's look at an example...

Suppose you have a **Main Menu** button, and its function is to take the user back to the card named `main`. Having this as the button's script would seem to make sense:

```
on mouseUp
    go card "main"
end mouseUp
```

It would appear to be the lowest level the code can be, and we're not going to be duplicating it, there's just one **Main Menu** button. But, suppose we want to track the user's progress, the **Main Menu** button won't know anything about that. So, we could do this instead:

```
on mouseUp
    navTo "main"
end mouseUp
```

In the card script there would be this handler:

```
on navTo aCard
    saveNavState
    go card aCard
end navTo
```

`saveNavState` would be a function somewhere that does the saving of the user's state. The only problem is that each of the cards we make that includes the **Main Menu** button will have to have this `navTo` handler in their scripts. Therefore, we'll put the handler into the mainstack stack script. With it at that level it can handle calls from any button on any card. The Help button's script could be:

```
on mouseUp
    navTo "help"
end mouseUp
```

Going to the Help card would also save the user's state. Later we could add a visual effect as you jump from place to place, and can make that change in `navTo`, instead of having to go to all of the various buttons that make use of the `navTo` handler.

Pop quiz – name that structure

1. There is a common term used to describe the LiveCode hierarchy that helps convey how information is passed up and down the hierarchy. What is that term?

    a. The Event Horizon

    b. The Message Path

    c. The Call Stack

    d. The Home Stack

Loading and saving external data

In many applications you will want to keep track of changes that the user has made. There are several ways to do that with LiveCode, including querying of a URL, reading and writing to a text file, and saving data inside a stack.

Querying a URL

Quite often web-based applications will load and save data from server side scripts. That can be done with LiveCode apps too. Here's an example, where we want to know what the closing price was for Google yesterday:

```
put url "http://quote.yahoo.com/d/quotes.csv?s=GOOG&f=p"
```

At the moment that line was tested, **609.46** appeared in the Message Box:

Who knows what you'll find when you try it!

As with any such calls to an online service there is a chance that it may take some time to return the value, and in the above example LiveCode would be blocked from doing anything else until the data was returned. An alternate approach would be to load the URL in order to cache it, and then display the results when it is cached. LiveCode would be able to do other actions while the data is being returned. A button script would look like this:

```
on mouseUp
   unload url "http://quote.yahoo.com/d/quotes.csv?s=GOOG&f=p"
   load url "http://quote.yahoo.com/d/quotes.csv?s=GOOG&f=p" with
message "gotit"
end mouseUp

on gotit addr, state
   if state is "cached" or state is "downloaded" then
      answer url addr
   else
      answer state
   end if
end gotit
```

The gotit handler also checks to see if the call worked, and if it didn't will display what the error was. The unload line is to make sure that you're not reading the previously cached value. If it's a value that will only change infrequently, as with the closing price of a stock, you would usually only clear the cached version when it's likely to have changed. On the next financial market day in this case.

Posting data can work in the same way. A game that sends your score in to the server could do it this way:

```
on sendscore username,score
    put url "http://www.mysite.com/hiscores/savescore.php?user=" &
username & "&score=" & score into err
    if err is not "ok" then answer err
end sendscore
```

If the username or any other parts of the data being posted contains space characters you would want to URLEncode the location first. Doing so will convert spaces and other special characters into codes that will safely arrive at the destination URL. This would be a safer variation:

```
on sendscore username,score
    put "http://www.mysite.com/hiscores/savescore.php?user=" &
username & "&score=" & score into tPostAddress
put url URLEncode(tPostAddress) into err
    if err is not "ok" then answer err
end sendscore
```

Reading and writing to a text file

Back in the days of HyperCard the only real choice for saving and loading external data was to write a text file. LiveCode can of course do that too, and in some cases it may be the simplest solution. Configuration and preferences files are a couple of good examples where a small text file can be used to setup the application in the way the user wishes it to be.

As an example, say we have configuration text files, named `englishstrings.txt` and `frenchstrings.txt`, that were included in the **Copy Files** list of the **Standalone Application Settings** dialog, and they are going to be used to set whether button names are in English or French within your application. We'll also want to write a preferences file to remember the user's choice. When the app is opened we would check to see what the preferences file says, and then load the appropriate strings file.

 With mobile operating systems, and iOS in particular, there are strict rules about where you are allowed to save data. As we move forward we will use locations that are approved for such use by Apple and Google.

Text files that you include in a mobile app will be in the same location as the app itself, and text files you want to write to should be in the `documents` folder for your app. Because those paths may look quite different on iOS and Android, we should use LiveCode's `specialFolderPath` function to locate those folders. Here's how an `openStack` handler would check to see if the preferences have been set, and if not, take the user to an initial language choice screen:

```
on openStack
   global langstrings
   put "file:" & specialFolderPath("documents") & "/prefs.txt" into
prefsfile
   put url prefsfile into prefstext
   if prefstext is empty then
      -- prefs have never been set, so go to the language choice card
      go card "language choice"
   else
      -- language has previously been chosen, so we load up the right
file
      put "file:" & specialFolderPath("engine") & prefstext &
"strings.txt" into langfile
      put url langfile into langstrings
   end if
end openStack
```

The engine special folder path is the same location as the application file, and also the supporting files that you included in the **Copy Files** section of the **Standalone Application Settings** dialog (as described in the **Copy Files** topic in *Chapter 7*), when saving the standalone application. In the above example there would be files named `englishstrings.txt`, `frenchstrings.txt`, `spanishstrings.txt`, and so on. This line:

```
put "file:" & specialFolderPath("engine") & prefstext & "strings.txt"
into langfile
```

will concatenate the path to where the included files are located, the language that you wish to use (stored in the variable `prefstext`), and the ending of those file names. This will give the full path to the language strings text file that matches your chosen language.

Using another stack to store data

Ideally you would just save changes into the stack you are in at the time, except that iOS doesn't permit saving into the application directory. We have to work around that, by saving a stack into the documents folder. The stack to save can either be the one that is our application stack, or it could just be one used purely for storing data. Saving data in a stack can be more convenient than saving to text files. For example, you can have several text fields that are there just to store bits of information that will be needed the next time the app is run. If you were using text files you would either need lots of them, or you will have to process the text from a single file in order to extract the individual bits of information.

It's possible to try out saving data in stacks without making a mobile app, to see if the basic technique works, and then afterwards try it on an actual device. An advantage to trying it on your computer first is that you can browse to the documents folder, in order to see the magic as it happens!

Time for action – creating a data save stack

We're going to be making a copy of a stack, but only if a copy of the stack doesn't already exist. LiveCode has a nice "if there is a..." function, which was made for times like this!

Firstly we will create the stacks we'll need.

1. Start a new **Mainstack**, with a name of `LaunchStack`. Save it somewhere other than your computer's **Documents** folder.

2. Start another new **Mainstack**, with a name of `AppStack`. Save it next to the first stack.

3. Place something onto each stack's card, so you can easily recognize when you're in that stack. For example, drag a button onto the card of the `LaunchStack` stack and name it in a way that makes it very easy to tell where you are. Do the same for the `AppStack` stack.

4. Put this `openStack` handler into the stack script of `LaunchStack`:

```
on openStack
    set the defaultFolder to specialFolderPath("Documents")
    if there is not a file "AppStack.livecode" then
        put the filename of this stack into masterfile
        set the itemdelimiter to "/"
        put "AppStack.livecode" into the last item of masterfile
        --put specialFolderPath("engine") & "/AppStack.livecode"
into masterfile
        put specialFolderPath("Documents") & "/AppStack.livecode"
into appfile
```

```
      put URL ("binfile:" & masterfile) into URL ("binfile:" &
appfile)
   end if
   go stack specialFolderPath("Documents") & "/AppStack.livecode"
answer the filename of this stack
end openStack
```

5. Save both stacks, and quit LiveCode.

Before trying the stacks on a device or in the simulator, we'll try them as desktop stacks.

1. Look in your `Documents` folder, and there should not be an `AppStack.livecode` file at the moment.

2. Launch LiveCode by double clicking on the `LaunchStack.livecode` file. If you find that LiveCode doesn't launch this way, make sure you have associated `.livecode` documents to be opened by LiveCode.

3. Look in your `Documents` folder, and there now should be an `AppStack.livecode` file, with a created time that matches the current time.

4. You should also see that the path to the **AppStack** is indeed in your `Documents` folder.

Now to try it on a mobile device, or by using the iOS Simulator.

1. Close the **AppStack** stack, and uncomment the **put specialFolderPath...** line from the **LaunchStack** stack script that you entered at step 4.

2. Go into **Standalone Application Settings**, and choose the **Copy Files** section.

3. Click on **Add File...** and locate and add the original `AppStack.livecode` stack (not the one that was created with the previous test).

4. Choose either the **Android** or **iOS** section of the **Standalone Application Settings**, and check the box to create the app for that platform.

5. From the **Development** menu, select your test target. That would be either one of the iOS simulators if you chose **iOS**, or a connected Android device.

6. Select **Test** from the **Development** menu. You should end up with your AppStack showing, and an alert dialog showing the path to the stack. The following screenshot shows the resulting dialog in the iOS Simulator window and in an Android 4 tablet:

What just happened?

We set up our app to copy the main application stack into the documents area on the device, so that we'll be able to make changes and save those successfully. If you happened to test on iOS and Android you will have seen quite different looking paths for the stack. LiveCode takes care of finding those special folders for us.

Pop quiz – other special places

1. See if you just happen to know this, or use this question as an excuse to read the release notes and the dictionary! Which of these is NOT a `specialFolderPath` type?

    a. Users

    b. Home

    c. Desktop

    d. 0x000e

Creating a web "scraper" app

As an excuse to try out various native mobile controls, we're going to make an app that can read web pages and extract links to the different media on the page. The app will have a card that shows a web browser, cards for showing the links, text, and media from the web page, and a set of cards for remembering selected items.

Time for action – setting up tab navigation

Before getting into making the Browser card, we need to set up the items that are shared across all of the cards in the app.

1. Create a new **Mainstack**, set its name to `WebScraper`, and save it somewhere.

2. We'll use MobGUI again, to make life easier. Select **revMobGUI** from the **Development/Plugins** submenu.

3. In these instructions we'll use iPhone, portrait, but feel free to use iPad or an Android size for the card. Select either **iPhone and Portrait** in the **MobGUI** window, or your preferred options.

4. Uncheck the **Status** bar box.

5. As you did in the *Time for action – using MobGUI to remember layouts for us* from *Chapter 3, Building User Interfaces* use the MobGUI tools to add a NavBar (which will snap to the top of the card window), a BG to set the nice background pattern, and a TabBar, that will snap to the bottom of the card window.

6. Right-click on the **Tab** button control in the MobGUI window, and choose **5** from the drop-down menu. Drag the five buttons to the card.

7. Option/*Alt*+double-click on one of the five buttons to make them spread across the card window, and nudge them up or down to rest centered on the TabBar.

8. Give the five buttons the names `BrowserButton`, `Links`, `Text`, `Media`, and `Keepers`.

8. Edit the script of each button, and in the `touchStart` handler, add a `pass` `touchStart` line, to leave the handler looking like this:

    ```
    on touchStart pId
       mobGUITouch the long id of me
       pass touchStart
    end touchStart
    ```

9. Set the name of the **NavBar** to `NavBar`.

10. From the **Edit menu**, **Select All**, and **Group Selected** from the **Object** menu.

11. Edit the script of the group you just formed, and enter this script:

```
on touchStart
    put the uTabText of me into tTabText
    set the uText of group "NavBar" to tTabText
    go card tTabText
init
end touchStart
```

12. Select the group, and in the regular LiveCode **Object Inspector Basic Settings** give the group a name of Common, and check the **Behave like a background** button.

13. Set the name of the card to **Browser**.

14. In the MobGUI window, click the **Add preOpenCard** code to card script button.

15. Make a new card, name it Links, and click the **Add preOpenCard** button again.

16. Do the same for three more cards, to be named Text, Media, and Keepers.

17. Go into **Standalone Application Settings**, choose **iOS** or **Android** as the platform you want to use, select the appropriate target from the **Development** menu, and do a **Test**.

18. Click or touch on the five tab buttons, and you should see the name of the NavBar change, and the highlighted tab button should be the one you clicked on.

What just happened?

In naming the buttons and the cards the same, we were able to go to the five cards using the script attached to the group. Also, we used the MobGUI uTabText and uText properties to set the name of the NavBar to match the name of the card we had jumped to. The init line will come into its own as we write the card scripts.

The Browser card

Now we'll add a few controls and scripts to the first card, to create this mini web browser:

LiveCode has, at the time of writing, been updated so that the features on Android match the features on iOS. Unfortunately, MobGUI has not been updated in the same way. The native browser control only works on iOS. It is to be hoped that MobGUI will be updated soon!

The native browser control has many properties, actions, and messages associated with it, and you should read the latest release notes to see the full list. You can open both the **iOS Release Notes** and the **Android Release Notes** from the LiveCode **Help** menu. For our application though, we will only need a few of its abilities.

Time for action – adding the browser controls

Return to the first card of the stack, and find your way to the native controls part of the MobGUI window.

1. Drag the Browser control onto the card window. It's the one with the thumbnail showing Google's search page.

2. Resize the control to fill the width of the card, and its height to fit between the tab bar and a little way below the NavBar. Give it the name **Browser**.

3. With the browser control selected, check the box in the MobGUI window titled **Auto destroy on closeCard**. This will help reduce the memory usage of the final app during the times you're not on the browser card.

4. Drag a native **Text** control into the gap between the browser control and the NavBar. Name it `url`, and resize it to be nearly as wide as the card, leaving space for a **Go** button on the right.

5. Drag a **Button** control into that space, set its label to `Go`, and resize it to look nice. You can **Option**/*Alt*-double-click to have it space itself a standard distance from the right of the card window.

6. Edit the script of the **Go** button (which as you may notice is really a group), and add a couple of lines before the end of the `touchStart` handler, like so:

```
--other lines are here
set the uURL of group "Browser" to the uText of group "url"
focus on nothing
end touchEnd
```

7. Later we will be sending an `init` message to the cards. For the Browser card we can use that as a way to restore the previously chosen web page:

```
on init
   global gPageURL
   if gPageURL is not empty then
      set the uURL of group "Browser" to gPageURL
   else
      set the uURL of group "Browser" to "http://www.google.com/"
   end if
end init
```

8. Edit the script of the browser control. We're going to use the `browserFinishedLoading` message to know when to update some variables and URL text.

9. Add this handler to the bottom of the browser control's script:

```
on browserFinishedLoading pURL,pType
    global gPageURL,gPageHTML
    put pURL into gPageURL
    put url pURL into gPageHTML
    set the uText of group "url" to pURL
end browserFinishedLoading
```

10. Do a **Save**, and another **Test**, to see the browser card in action.

What just happened?

Setting the uURL of the browser control to the uText of the **Text** control was enough to make the browser function, but some of what was just done was in preparation for what we'll need in the other cards. In particular, we used the regular LiveCode put url command to stash a copy of the web page HTML code into a global variable, and that will be needed when we start to extract links and media from the page.

The Links card

The Links, Text, and Media cards are going to take the page source that is stored in the gPageHTML global variable, and extract the bits of interest from it. How will it do that?

A common approach when extracting a known pattern of text is to use regular expressions, often referred to as **regex** or **regexp**. At its simplest it's easy to understand, but it can get quite complex. Read the Wikipedia article if you want to understand it in depth:

http://en.wikipedia.org/wiki/Regular_expression

Another useful source of information is this Packt article on regular expressions:

http://www.packtpub.com/article/regular-expressions-python-26-text-processing

One problem though is that using regexp to parse HTML content is frowned upon. There are scores of articles online telling you outright not to parse HTML with regexp! Here's one pithy example:

http://boingboing.net/2011/11/24/why-you-shouldnt-parse-html.html

Now, parsing HTML source is exactly what we want to do here, and one solution to the problem is to mix and match, using LiveCode's other text matching and filtering abilities to do most of the work. Although it's not exactly regexp, LiveCode can use regular expressions in some of its matching and filtering functions, and they are somewhat easier to understand than full-blown regexp. So, let's begin by using those ...

In looking for links we will make the assumption that the link is inside an `a href` tag, but even then there are a lot of variations of how that can appear. The general structure of an a href tag is like this:

```
<a href="http://www.runrev.com/support/forum/">Link text that the user
will see</a>
```

In the text of the web page will be the phrase **Link text that the user will see**. If the user places their cursor over that text, the cursor will change to be a pointing finger cursor. When the link text is clicked, the page will reload using the URL shown in the `href` part of the tag.

The above example shows the full path to the support forum. Here are some of the ways that the very same web location might be written in a page link:

```
http://www.runrev.com/support/forum/
```

/support/forum/

support/forum/

../support/forum/

The first will take you there no matter where you are at the time. The second will take you there if you're somewhere else on the runrev.com site. The third will be correct while you are at the root level of runrev.com, and the last example would work from within one of the other root level directories on the site.

With regex you might create an extravagant expression that deals with all possible variations of how the links are contained in the page source, but even then it would not give us the full paths we need.

Taking things slowly, we can reduce the whole page source to a set of lines of `a href` entries, then extract the URL part of each line, and finally take the above variations and convert them into full path URLs.

Time for action – making a links extraction function

Sometimes it's handy to create tests in a separate stack, and then to copy the function you've made into your application stack.

1. Create a new **Mainstack**. Save it, just to be safe!

2. Add a couple of fields and a button.

3. Set the button's script to this:

```
on mouseUp
    put url "http://www.runrev.com/" into field 1
    put getLinks(field 1) into field 2
end mouseUp
```

4. Edit the stack script, and create a function for `getLinks`. Start with it just returning what it's sent:

```
function getLinks pPageSource
    return pPageSource
end getLinks
```

5. If you were to try clicking on the button at this point, you will see that the whole page source appears in field 2.

6. We're going to use the filter function, and that needs the text to be in separate lines. So we want each link to be in a line of its own. The replace function can do that nicely. Add these two lines to the script (before the `return` line, of course!):

```
replace "/a>" with "/a>" & return in pPageSource

replace "<a" with return & "<a" in pPageSource
```

7. Try clicking on the button. The two fields will look much the same, but any lines that have a link in them will be on a line of their own.

8. Add a line to filter the list as it stands, to reduce it to just the ones with links in them:

```
filter pPageSource with "*a href */a>"
```

9. The "*" characters are wildcards, making the list reduce to lines that contain both `a href` and `/a>`. Try the button again.

10. Now you'll see that there are only lines with links in them, but they still include the junk on either side of the link itself. The part we need is between the first and second quote marks, and using the itemdelimiter we can get at that bit. Add these lines:

```
set the itemdelimiter to quote
    repeat with a = 1 to the number of lines in pPageSource
        put item 2 of line a of pPageSource into line a of
pPageSource
    end repeat
```

11. When you now click on the button you should get a list of only the URL part of each line. But notice that most of the links start with /, and not `http`.

12. Make another function in the stack script that will change the links to be full path:

```
function getPath pPageURL,pLinkURL
end getPath
```

13. Now add the code needed to cope with the URL variations, starting with the case where it's a full path:

```
if pLinkURL contains "://" then
    return pLinkURL
end if
```

14. If you recall, earlier we saved the URL of the main page in a global variable, gPageURL. For the case where the link is root relative (it starts with a "/") we want to combine the host location and the link URL:

```
set the itemdelimiter to "/"
if char 1 of pLinkURL is "/" then
    return item 1 to 3 of pPageURL & pLinkURL
else
```

15. When that first character is not "/", it may start with "../" to step up one level in the directory structure. Deleting the last part of the page URL will give us what we need to combine with the link URL:

```
if char 1 to 3 of pLinkURL is "../" then
        delete the last item of pPageURL
        delete the last item of pPageURL
        delete char 1 to 2 of pLinkURL
        return pPageURL & pLinkURL
        else
```

16. For other cases we combine the page URL and the link URL:

```
delete the last item of pPageURL
        return pPageURL & "/" & pLinkURL
        end if
    end if
```

17. Lastly, if all of those checks failed we will return an empty string, so that this strange structured link URL doesn't go on to confuse us later:

```
    return ""
end getPath
```

18. To get the `getLinks` function to use the `getPath` function we need to make a change to the script shown in step 10:

```
repeat with a = 1 to the number of lines in pPageSource
     put getPath(gPageURL,item 2 of line a of pPageSource) into
line a of pPageSource
   end repeat
```

What just happened?

In stages we developed a function that can find the links in a web page's source text, finishing with a set of full path URLs that we can present to the user.

The missing links

The one missing piece in the test stack is the global variable that stores the page URL. In the case of the app stack, that value is provided by the browser control's `browserFinishedLoading` function, but here we need to plug in a value for testing purposes.

Place a global declaration line in the button script and in the stack script. In the button script, fill in the variable with our test case value. The script will then look like this:

```
global gPageURL

on mouseUp
   put "http://www.runrev.com/" into gPageURL
   put url gPageURL into field 1
   put getLinks(field 1) into field 2
end mouseUp
```

If you try the button now, you should see a list of 12 full path URLs in your second field. If it works correctly, copy the two stack functions, and the global declaration line, and paste them into the stack script of the WebScraper stack.

One more thing...

The tab bar script included a line `init`. That will call into the card script, in this case, the Links card script. But that doesn't exist yet! Let's make it.

Time for action – adding the Links card "init" handler

Before proceeding, make sure you are happy with the functions in the test stack, and that you have copied them to the WebScraper stack script.

1. Go to the **Links** card of the **WebScraper** stack.

2. In the **MobGUI** window, click on the **Add preOpenCard** script button.

3. Edit the card script, and add these global variables and `init` function:

```
global gPageHTML,gLinks

on init
  if the platform is "iphone" or the platform is "android" then
      put getLinks(gPageHTML) into gLinks
      if the number of lines in gLinks = 0 then
          answer "There are no links in this page!"
      else
          mobilePick gLinks,0
          if the result > 0 then
              put the result into tLinkLine
              put line tLinkLine of gLinks into tLink
              go card "Browser"
              set the uText of group "url" to tLink
              set the uText of group "NavBar" to "Browser"
              set the uURL of group "Browser" to the uText of group
"url"
              mobGUITouch the long id of group "BrowserButton"
          end if
      end if
    end if
end init
```

4. Do a **Test** of the app.

5. In the iPhone Simulator, or Android device if that's what you're using, change the URL to `http://www.runrev.com/`, and select the **Go** button.

6. When the page is loaded, select the Links tab button.

7. You should now be looking at that list of 12 links, only this time it's presented in a native picker list.

8. Select the third link in the list, and then **Done**.

9. You should be taken back to the **Browser** card, with RunRev's Facebook page loaded.

What just happened?

The card script we entered does the same job as the button in the test stack, in that it calls to the stack functions to get a list of links. Rather than putting the list into a plain field, we used LiveCode's ability to open a native picker control, by using the line:

```
mobilePick gLinks,0
```

The required parameters of that function are a list of items to show, and the index position of the one to be selected. By entering 0 there is in effect no item selected. The result that comes back from the picker is the index position of the item that was selected, and we can use that to look up the matching line in the gLinks variable.

The remaining lines take us back to the Browser card, set the URL to be loaded, and also make sure the **BrowserButton** tab button is highlighted.

The Text card

Making the Text card work will be a lot simpler, but will include an unbelievably complex regular expression line, as given on this web page:

```
http://stackoverflow.com/questions/3951485/regex-extracting-readable-
non-code-text-and-urls-from-html-documents
```

Time for action – setting up the Text card

Start off in the test stack you made, so we can get the function working there before adding it to the WebScraper stack.

1. Duplicate the button you made when extracting links. Change the function call getLinks to say getText - otherwise the script can remain the same.

2. Edit the script of the test stack, and add this function:
```
function getText pPageSource
    put replaceText(pPageSource,"(?:<(?P<tag>script|style)
[\s\S]*?</(?P=tag)>)|(?:<!--[\s\S]*?-->)|(?:<[\s\S]*?>)","") into
pPageSource
    replace lf with "" in pPageSource
    replace tab with " " in pPageSource
    return pPageSource
end getText
```

3. Try clicking on the button you just made. You should see your second field fill with just the text parts of the web page.

4. Copy the function, and go back to the WebScraper stack script. Paste the function there.

5. Go to the Text card of the stack, and from the MobGUI window drag a **Multiline Text** control onto the card. Set its name to PageText.

6. Resize the control to fill the area between the NavBar and the TabBar.

7. In the MobGUI window properties for the control, uncheck the box for **Editable**.

8. Edit the card script, and add this `init` function:

```
global gPageHTML

on init
    if the platform is "iphone" or the platform is "android" then
        mobFieldSet "PageText","text",getText(gPageHTML)
    end if
end init
```

9. Try a **Test** of the app.

10. In the Browser card, change the URL from google.com to runrev.com, and press **Go**.

11. Press the **Text** tab button at the bottom.

12. You should now be on the Text card, and seeing the text elements from the web page shown in a native scrolling text field.

What just happened?

That enormously long regular expression ran through the web page source and removed anything that was script, style, or just tag information, leaving the text parts alone. But that leaves it with lots of spare line feed characters and tab characters, which we went on to remove using the LiveCode replace function. The final text may not be perfect, but you can use the standard mobile text features to copy parts of it for use in other apps.

The Media card

The Media card is going to start off very much like the Links card, with an "init" function in the card script, and a stack script function to extract the media links from the page.

Time for action – extracting a list of media links

There probably is a regular expression that would extract all of the "src" links from a page, but we're only interested in things that we know LiveCode is able to show or play. So this time we'll use a more devious way to extract just the links we can handle.

1. You may as well head over to the test stack!

2. Make a third button by duplicating one of the other two, and change the `getLinks` or `getText` part in the button script to call `getMedia` instead.

3. In the stack script, enter all of this:

```
global gPageURL

function getMedia pPageSource
    put ".jpg,.png,.gif,.jpeg,.mov,.mp4,m4v,.mp3" into tExtensions
    repeat with a = 1 to the number of items in tExtensions
        put item a of tExtensions into tExtension
        replace tExtension with tExtension & "*" & return in
pPageSource
    end repeat
    repeat with a = the number of lines in pPageSource down to 1
        put line a of pPageSource into tLine
        if the last char of tLine is "*" then
            delete the last char of tLine
            put removeLeaders(gPageURL,tLine) into line a of
pPageSource
        else
            delete line a of pPageSource
        end if
    end repeat
    return pPageSource
end getMedia

function removeLeaders pPageURL,pLinkURL
    put quote&"'()" into tDelimiters
    repeat with a = 1 to the number of chars in tDelimiters
        put char a of tDelimiters into tDelimiter
        set the itemdelimiter to tDelimiter
        put the last item of pLinkURL into pLinkURL
    end repeat
    return getPath(pPageURL,pLinkURL)
end removeLeaders
```

4. Click on the button, and you should see a list of full paths to the various images in the web page.

What just happened?

The devious approach involved finding anywhere that any media of interest was mentioned and adding an asterisk and return character in order to make sure that the link was easily identified, and at the end of a unique line. Then each of those lines was sent to another function, removeLeaders, to remove any other text that was earlier in the line than the start of the link. Finally, the same getPath function we used when extracting links was used to give us full paths to the media files.

Now that we have a list of media links we will need to add the card level handlers required to present the list to the user, and to load their selected media item into the card window.

Time for action – setting up the Media card scripts

Copy the functions you proved to work in the test stack script, and paste them into WebScraper stack script. Then...

1. Go to the Media card. As with the Links card we're not going to add any controls to the card, we'll do that with script. So, edit the card script.

2. Here is the Media card's `init` function, and needed global variables:

```
global gPageHTML,gMediaList

on init
    if the platform is "iphone" or the platform is "android" then
        put getMedia(gPageHTML) into gMediaList
        if the number of lines in gMediaList = 0 then
            answer "There is no media in this page!"
        else
            set the itemdelimiter to "/"
            put empty into tMediaNames
            repeat with a = 1 to the number of lines in gMediaList
                put the last item of line a of gMediaList into line a
of tMediaNames
            end repeat
            mobilePick tMediaNames,1
            if the result > 0 then
                put the result into tMediaLine
                showMedia line tMediaLine of gMediaList
            end if
        end if
    end if
end init
```

3. Unlike the Links case, we build up a list of just the file name part of the URL, to show in a native picker, and when you've selected something we call a `showMedia` function in the stack script.

4. Edit the stack script.

5. Create the showMedia function:

```
on showMedia pMediaFile
    if there is an image "mediaImage" then delete image
"mediaImage"
    set the itemdelimiter to "."
    switch (the last item of pMediaFile)
        case "png"
        case "gif"
        case "jpg"
        case "jpeg"
            new image
            set the name of image the number of images to
"mediaImage"
            set the filename of image "mediaImage" to pMediaFile
            break
        case "mp4"
        case "m4v"
        case "mov"
        case "mp3"
            set the showController of the templatePlayer to true
            play video pMediaFile
            break
    end switch
end showMedia
```

6. **Test** the app.

7. You can start with the google.com page, press the **Media** tab button to see a list of the images used on that page.

8. Select an image from the list, and press **Done**.

9. The image should appear on the card.

10. Go back to the Browser card, and change the URL to http://www.apple.com/.

11. Apple usually includes some video link thumbnails on the main page. Press on one of those, so that you see the large video player. But don't play it!

12. Press the **Media** tab button, to see a list of all of the media on that page.

13. Scroll down the list, looking for one of the longer named items, that seems like it might be that video.

14. Select that item and press **Done**. The video should load and play on the card.

15. Use the video controller's **Done** button when you are finished watching the video, to return to the Media card.

16. You can press the **Media** tab button again to make the picker reappear.

17. Go back to the Browser card, and enter a URL that contains examples of MP3 files. `http://www.ntonyx.com/mp3_songs.htm` is one such example.

18. Press the **Media** tab button to return to the Media card, with the list of all of the media on that page, which in this case will be mainly MP3 files.

19. Select one of the MP3s from the list, and press **Done**. The MP3 should play in the same player that the video played in.

What just happened?

In this example we made use of both a standard LiveCode control, the image, and also a native control, the video player. LiveCode handles the setting up of the player, and with the very simple `play video videoname` syntax, we were able to invoke the native player. It was able to play both video and audio files.

The Keepers card

Actually, it's going to be the Keepers cards. These are to be a place you can stash media that you found interesting. For file size reasons we're actually just going to store the URL to the media - after all a long video would soon use up your device's storage!

Time for Action – setting up the Keepers card

As the Keepers card is at the end of the stack, you can get to it with either repeated **View/Go Next** actions, or just a single **View/Go Last** action.

1. Go to the Keepers card, and create a MobGUI button for **Prev**, **Next**, and **Play Media**. Make a LiveCode field, and name it `mediaURL`. You should now have something looking like this:

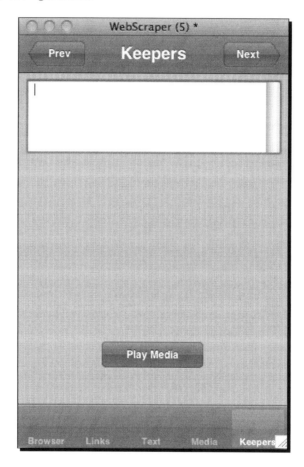

2. Add these lines to the `touchStart` handler of the **Prev** button:

```
if the name of this card is not "Keepers" then
    go previous
end if
```

3. Add these lines to the `touchStart` handler of the **Next** button:

```
if the number of this card < the number of cards then
   go next
end if
```

4. Add this line to the **Play Media** button's `touchStart` handler:

```
showMedia field "mediaURL"
```

5. Select those four controls and Group them. Check the box that says **Behave like a background**. Name the group as `keeperbuttons`.

6. Edit the script of the new group. Add this `refresh` handler:

```
on refresh
   set the itemdelimiter to "."
   if char 1 of the last item of field "mediaURL" is "m" then
      show group "Play Media"
   else
      hide group "Play Media"
      showMedia field "mediaURL"
   end if
end refresh
```

7. Now we need to go back and add some things to the Media card.

8. Go to the Media card, and add a MobGUI button. Set the name and label to `Keep Media`.

9. One tricky thing is that media will play full screen on smaller screens, and by the time you see the Keep Media button the video has already gone away. We can work around that by storing the URL of the last shown media item in a global variable.

10. In the Media card script, change the `init` function so that the later lines read:

```
if the result > 0 then
        put the result into tMediaLine
        put line tMediaLine of gMediaList into gLastMedia
        showMedia gLastMedia
    end if
```

11. Change the global variable declaration line to include the `gLastMedia` variable.

12. Set the `touchStart` handler of the **Keep Media** button to be:

```
on touchStart pId
   global gLastMedia
   mobGUITouch the long id of me
   go last card
   if field "mediaURL" is not empty then
      new card
   end if
   put gLastMedia into field "mediaURL"
      save stack "WebScraper"
      send "refresh" to group "keeperbuttons"
end touchStart
```

13. **Test** the app. Use the Browser card to load a page with plenty of images, videos, or sounds on it, and go to the Media card to see those listed.

14. Select any item, followed by **Done**.

15. If you like the image, sound, or video, use the **Keep Media** button to go to the end of the stack for the media's URL to be saved.

16. Choose more bits of media, and keep them.

17. Go to the **Keepers** section and use the **Next** and **Prev** buttons to browse through the items you kept.

18. The images should appear automatically, and the video and audio can be started with the **Play Media** button.

What just happened?

We added the last feature of our application, a set of cards where we can go to view the bits of media that we chose to keep.

Have a go hero – add some preset locations

If you do make the WebScraper app, and start to find it useful, it's quite likely that there will be a set of web pages that you go back to over and over. Having to type in the URL every time would be tedious. So, why not make a hidden field on the Browser card, and type in a list of your favorite pages. Add a button to the card too, that will bring up a list of those pages for you to choose from. The one you choose can then load the Browser control with the desired page. All of the steps to do this were covered in *The Links card* section above.

What now?

It's pretty certain that if you carefully followed all of the steps in this chapter, and indeed that all of the steps were perfect, you still wouldn't have an app ready to be submitted to the app stores! There should be a splash screen, a main menu, and icons on the tab buttons. Some love from a graphic designer! Feature wise it would be nice if the images you keep could be zoomed and panned.

Summary

Some of what we covered here is less glamorous, mostly about processing HTML text, but we did also use a few mobile features, including:

- Making and controlling a web browser
- Using a native picker to present lists
- Creating a native scrolling field, that has all of the normal OS specific abilities
- Playing video and audio using the native media player

The next chapter is almost entirely about dealing with graphics, so we'll make sure to use some image manipulating gestures, and you could revisit the WebScraper app later to add the same features to the Keepers cards.

5
Making a Jigsaw Puzzle Application

Picture this...

So far we've been dealing with a lot of text, or calling on mobile OS features. Those are neat things, but they're not that visual. If you were longing to mess around with pictures and image data, your time has come!

LiveCode isn't naturally a graphics powerhouse, and its way of handling image data (often referred to as "bitmap data" by other tools) is somewhat unusual, in that it effectively stores the pixels of an image as a series of single byte characters to represent the red, green, and blue values of each pixel. Handling of a final image is quite flexible, but in order to create something along the lines of a jigsaw puzzle we need to understand the image data format.

In this chapter we will cover the following:

- ◆ Examine the way that LiveCode stores bitmap data in an image object
- ◆ Find a way to use a single bitmap in place of 50 buttons
- ◆ Make a collision detection map
- ◆ Create a jigsaw puzzle app that takes advantage of several mobile device features

Image data format

In other authoring tools, such as Adobe Director and Adobe Flash, bitmap data is stored as a matrix of 24- or 32-bit values. If you want to know the color of the 20th pixel from the left-hand edge, in the 15th row from the top of the image, you would use a `getPixel` function with those numbers plugged in. In Flash, which uses a zero starting point for all of its variable types, you would say:

```
pixelcolor = bitmapvariable.getPixel(19,14);
```

You would in fact start that line with `var pixelcolor:uint`, but here we're looking at the main differences, and not the oddities of having a strongly typed programming language! In Director, which, like LiveCode, uses 1 based variables, you would say:

```
pixelcolor = imagevariable.getPixel(20,15)
```

Again there's no need for variable typing, or even a semicolon at the end of the line. While we digress, Flash also doesn't need the semicolon at the end; at least, you don't have to type it yourself. Flash knew what you meant! Getting back to the point...

In LiveCode each pixel of an image is represented by four bytes, which you access as if they are single-byte characters. The range of values in a byte is 0-255, and storing such values, especially the value "0", in character variables does not work out well. Therefore, you must convert the character value into a numeric value before making use of it. The basic problem is that although the numeric value is stored in a variable, when you come to do calculations on it LiveCode will want to work in base 10 arithmetic, and not in the binary form inside the variable. You have to convert the variable into something that can be processed, using the `charToNum` function.

So why would a character variable not like zeros, you ask! Well, in the earliest days of personal computers the predominant programming language was Pascal. In Pascal a variable that contained a literal string needed to have a way to know how long the string was. The first byte of a Pascal string stores the length of the string, which was fine up to 255 characters, and in those days it was most likely thought of as being as much as anyone would ever need! In real life though, strings can be longer than 255 characters. This paragraph alone is over 900 characters long. To solve this issue the C programming language used a zero to indicate the end of a string. You could have a million characters in a row, however, only the last one would be a zero. RGB values don't care about the limitations of C strings, and there are zeros all over the place, which is why we convert it to a numeric value as soon as we can.

In addition to the oddity of each pixel being stored as four bytes of information, there's also no sense of rows and columns. All of the pixels in an image have their four bytes end to end, you have to do a calculation to know where in the data the pixel you're looking for is located. If you consider how you work in a bitmap editor, say Photoshop or Gimp, you select things based on an X and a Y value, which correspond to the column and row where the pixel is located in the image. LiveCode doesn't let you access bitmaps in that way. Hence the need to do a calculation.

Here's how the above example pixel would be retrieved in LiveCode, if you wanted it as a 24-bit value:

```
put getPixel("test image",20,15) into pixelcolor

function getPixel pImage,pX,pY
    put the imageData of image pImage into tImageData
    put the width of image pImage into tWidth
    put ((pY-1)*tWidth + (pX-1)) * 4 into tStartChar
    put charToNum(char tStartChar+2 of tImageData) into tRed
    put charToNum(char tStartChar+3 of tImageData) into tGreen
    put charToNum(char tStartChar+4 of tImageData) into tBlue
    return tRed*65536+tGreen*256+tBlue
end getPixel
```

On the face of it, this is one of the few cases where the way it's done in LiveCode is considerably longer than it is in other languages. However, quite often you really need the red, green, and blue values from the pixel, and in the other languages you have to take extra steps to extract those values.

The extra steps needed to make the returned number be a 24-bit RGB value are no big deal, seeing as LiveCode is easily extended by your own functions. If you need the 24-bit value, use the function above and you will have added a getPixel function to the LiveCode language. You do still have to do the calculations to get just the red value. Maybe one day LiveCode will have a built in getPixel function that works quicker than your own function. The 24-bit number returned here is in fact represented as three decimal numbers, not as a 24-bit binary value, but it would still be generally referred to as being "24 bit".

Mystery byte...

The first character of the four, which represents one pixel, is not used. RunRev.com has tutorials on how to use **imageData**, and there that byte is referred to as being Alpha. That makes sense, even the other tools that can give you a 32-bit number will have the value broken up into Alpha, Red, Green, and Blue. Why doesn't that byte, that RunRev themselves calls Alpha, contain the alpha value? Who knows!

One possibility is that the value didn't serve its purpose well enough. When talking about alpha transparency you sometimes mean that it's transparent, as might be the case in a GIF image. Other times you may mean translucent, where it's only partially see-through.

To solve the ambiguous nature of this problem, LiveCode has two other properties of an image, `maskData` and `alphaData`:

```
put the maskData of image "test image" into tMaskData
put the alphaData of image "test image" into tAlphaData
```

These properties of an image still have all of the rows end to end, and you still have to do the calculation to find where a given pixel's alpha value is stored.

With `maskData` you get a set of values for each of the pixels. For any value other than 0, the pixel is visible.

With `alphaData` you get a set of values representing the opaqueness of the pixel. 0 would be fully transparent, 255 would be fully opaque, and the values in between will be translucent. 128 would be 50% opaque.

Later in this chapter we are going to be making use of both `maskData` and `alphaData`, and we will refer to the 0-255 `alphaData` value as its **transparency**, and the zero or non-zero `maskData` value as its **mask**.

Misusing imageData!

The topics in the LiveCode online tutorials involve manipulation of the **imageData**, for example, turning a colored image into a grayscale one. (That particular example is located at: `http://lessons.runrev.com/s/lessons/m/4071/l/25371-vision-how-do-i-convert-a-color-image-to-grayscale`.) We're not going to do that here. Instead, we'll use the values in the image, the mask, and the alpha, to achieve some neat things that don't change the image at all. In fact, in some cases we won't even see the image!

Time for action – testing a getPixel function

Before getting to useful examples, let's make a `getPixel` function, and a quick test case.

1. Make a new **Mainstack**. **Save** it as `ImageDataTests`.

 We'll use the same stack to illustrate several things, and at the end we may dare to try it on a mobile device!

2. Make the stack of the size of your largest test device. Or just try 1024x768 if you'll use the iPad Simulator.

3. From the **File** menu, choose **Import as Control/Image,** and select any small image file you have, to place it in the upper left-hand side corner of the card window. The example shown below uses a LiveCode logo image.

4. Place a new **Graphic** object next to the image. It's going to be showing a single color, so just make it big enough to easily see the color. Name it `swatch`.

5. Graphics have a default value set to show an empty box, so type this in the message box to make it be filled in:

```
set the filled of graphic 1 to true
```

6. Edit the script of the image, and type in these lines:

```
on mouseMove pMx,pMy
    --put getPixel(the short name of me,pMx - the left of me,pMy -
the top of me) into tPixelColor
    --set the backgroundColor of graphic "swatch" to tPixelColor
end mouseMove
```

7. Note that two lines are commented out. LiveCode would only complain if we keep asking for `getPixel`, before we've created that function!

8. Edit the stack script. Add the `getPixel` function, which is very much like the one shown in the *Image data format* section earlier in this chapter:

```
function getPixel pImage,pX,pY
    put the imageData of image pImage into tImageData
    put the width of image pImage into tWidth
    put ((pY-1)*tWidth + (pX-1)) * 4 into tStartChar
    put charToNum(char tStartChar+2 of tImageData) into tRed
    put charToNum(char tStartChar+3 of tImageData) into tGreen
    put charToNum(char tStartChar+4 of tImageData) into tBlue
    return tRed,tGreen,tBlue
end getPixel
```

9. Back in the image script, uncomment the two lines. Start pointing at the image, and you should see the swatch graphic change color to match the pixel under the cursor

What just happened?

We made a very simple example case of using the color of a pixel in an image, in this case to color a swatch. As setting the `backgroundColor` of a graphic requires `redvalue,greenvalue,bluevalue`, we didn't need to convert the values from the image to a 24-bit number, and the `getPixel` function could return `tRed,tGreen,tBlue`.

Now, there isn't really any advantage to the way we did that as compared to the built in `mouseColor` function. But at least we gave the `getPixel` function a tryout!

Pop-Quiz – how many bits in a byte?

"Bytes" was mentioned a few times, and you may well know about "bit depth" when talking about digital photographs. How many bits are there in a byte?

    a.   32.

    b.   24.

    c.   8.

    d.   Depends on how hungry you are.

Simulating lots and lots of buttons

In some applications you need to know exactly which area of an image the user is pointing to. For example, when there is a map and you want to show information relating to the region the user has clicked on. That could be done using a lot of rectangular buttons, or you could break the regions up into graphics and use a `mouseEnter` handler to detect which region it is. Or instead you could use a single image to represent all of the regions.

Time for action – making a map of the United States

There are plenty of places online to get public domain images for use in your applications. Search for "public domain images", and you will see links to Wikipedia articles, government sites, and other sites dedicated to downloads of free-to-use images. The map shown here came from this file:

```
http://upload.wikimedia.org/wikipedia/commons/3/32/Blank_US_Map.svg
```

    1.   Make a new field named `states`. Find an alphabetical list of the 50 US states to paste into the field. Or type them in!

    2.   Make another field, set the text size to be 24, and the size of the field to be wide enough for "New Hampshire" to fit (just the words, not the entire state!). Name the field as `state`.

3. If you have Adobe Illustrator, open the SVG file. If not, open it with GIMP.

4. In alphabetical order, fill in each state with a color where the red, green, and blue values match the line number of that state + 100. We're adding 100 so that the shades of gray we'll see are not so black.

5. Continue through all of the states. Here's how it will start to look in Illustrator, where Idaho is about to be colored 112,112,112:

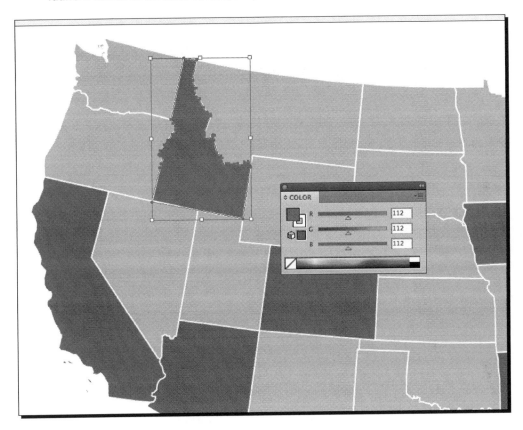

6. Change the size of the map so that it will fill about a third of the stack window, and choose **Export**.

Color profile settings

LiveCode treats bitmaps in a way that ignores color profile information in the image, and that would ruin what we're trying to do. When exporting an image see if there is an option to set the color profile to `genericRGB`. If there isn't, then use a utility such as Color Sync to apply the `genericRGB` color profile. Once the image is saved there is something you can do to make sure it gets imported into LiveCode: before doing the import, type `set the screengamma to 2.23` into the message box, and press *Enter*. This will set LiveCode to the right settings to make sure that the color values come in correctly.

7. If you're using Illustrator, set the background to be **White**, and the anti-aliasing to be **None**. With GIMP, make sure the PNG is saved without an alpha channel.

8. Type this line followed by the *Enter* key into the message box:

```
set the screengamma to 2.23
```

9. Import the PNG into your `ImageDataTests` stack.

10. Set the image's script to this:

```
on mouseMove pMx,pMy
    put getPixel(the short name of me,pMx - the left of me,pMy -
the top of me) into tStateColor
    set the itemdelimiter to comma
    put item 1 of tStateColor - 100 into tLine
    put line tLine of field "states" into field "state"
end mouseMove
```

11. Try pointing to the different states, at least the ones that you have colored in. The state name should appear in the `state` field.

What just happened?

For this case we only had to look at the value of the red channel for the pixel under the cursor. (The green and blue values are the same, because we used a gray color value.) Rather than write another function to get only the red part of the data, we reused the existing `getPixel` function, but then only took notice of the first item the function returned. That number, after subtracting the 100 that we added to make the shades not be so black, was then used as a lookup value to get the corresponding state name.

Pop-Quiz – getting the big picture

The example map image was an SVG file. Do a little Wikipedia research, and decide if an SVG file is smaller than a PNG file for a given image?

a. Yes.

b. No.

c. Depends on the nature of the image.

Using maskData for collision detection

In old 2D maze adventure games your character would move in distinct chunks, and when checking to see if there was a wall or a gap, the program had to check only relatively few locations. The occupied spots could be stored in an array, taking up little memory.

With other maze games, like those marble maze tilt boards, you have to detect collisions to a much finer degree. A full-blown physics engine could take care of the problem, but it's possible to get some interesting results by storing the maze as an image, and checking the pixels that are in front of your character, or marble as the case may be.

In a fully-featured game it would be better to use the `imageData`, or perhaps the `alphaData`, so that you can tell when you are going to hit something, and from the value you read you can also tell what it is you have hit. For example, in the marble maze game you need to know when you have gone over a hole.

For this next test though, we'll just use `maskData`, and see what we can do about not hitting the thing that is in front of us.

Time for action – making a racecourse

We're going to make a racecourse for little cars to move around. We'll make it out of the stack we've built! First we need to convert what is on the card into an image that represents walls and spaces.

1. Using the LiveCode draw tools, add a bunch of objects to the `ImageDataTest` stack. These are going to be obstacles in the racecourse.

2. To create the image we'll need, type this in the message box:

   ```
   import snapshot from rect the rect of this stack
   ```

3. The previous command will take a screenshot of the card window, and place it onto the card as a new image control.

4. Right-click on the image that was created, and select **Launch Editor**. This will open the image in the bitmap editor that you have set in **Preferences | General**.

5. In your image editor's **Layers** window, duplicate the initial single layer.

6. Make a new layer that is transparent, beneath the duplicate image layer.

7. Delete the original layer.

8. Use the editor's **Magic Wand** to select the white space of the card image in the layer with the image in it (not the transparent layer). Delete the selected area, to reveal the transparent layer.

9. Invert the selection, and fill it with a dark color (the color doesn't matter; it's just so we can see where the holes are).

10. Take some time to fill in any small gaps. Also, place a thick border around the outside of the image. The following screenshot shows how the card looks, and how the snapshot image should be by now:

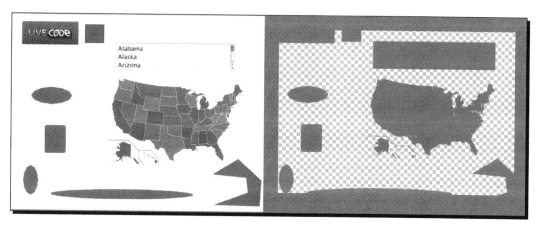

11. Merge the layers of the document, and then select **Save**.

12. Return to LiveCode, click on the **Update** button, and the snapshot image will be updated to reflect the changes you made.

13. Name the image as `backdrop`. Later we'll set the image to be behind other objects, but for now we'll leave it on top of everything else.

What just happened?

We just made a pretty strange looking racecourse! In a real top-down racing game you would carefully design a nice looking racecourse, and make a duplicate of the image to use for the collision detection. In the duplicate you would erase the parts of the image that represent where cars are allowed to drive, and then fill the rest of the image with a flat color. Players would see the nice looking racecourse, and underneath would be the duplicate flat color version used for detecting collisions.

We now need a car that drives itself around the course we've made.

Time for action – making a race car

Take as much time as you would like to create an image of the car. Make it so that it's facing to the right. Then once it's in the stack we'll start adding the required functions to its script. A size of about 40 pixels across should be about right. Here's a close up image of what we're talking about, as seen in Photoshop:

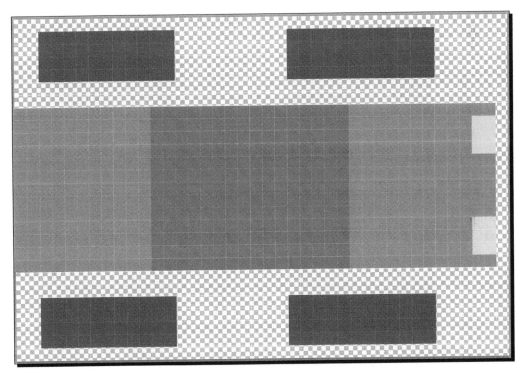

Yours can be even better than that, if you like! Save it as a 24-bit PNG that has transparency. Ok, start your engines...

1. Import the image as a control, and place it somewhere in the white area of the `ImageDataTests` stack. Name it `car1`.

2. Duplicate the image as many times as you like (the script below can handle up to 100 cars), and name each one in the following sequence, `car2`, `car3`, and so on.

3. Arguably, the correct object oriented way to proceed would be to place some functions on the images, and some in the card or stack script, but for performance reasons we'll put everything in the stack script. Open the stack script.

4. Add a line for the global variables we'll need:

```
global gBackdropMaskData,gMaskWidth,gSpeeds,gMovingCars,gMaskWidth
```

5. We'll add a start/stop button soon, which will call a function to toggle whether the cars are moving or not. Add the toggle function to the stack script:

```
on startStopCars
   if gMovingCars is true then
      put false into gMovingCars
   else
      put the maskData of image "backdrop" into gBackdropMaskData
      put the width of image "backdrop" into gMaskWidth
      setSpeeds
      put true into gMovingCars
      send moveCars to this card in 2 ticks
   end if
end startStopCars
```

6. The `setSpeeds` handler, which is called by `startStopCars`, will initialize the `gSpeeds` variable with a random speed for each of the car images. It will also set the initial direction to zero, as well as positioning the car at a known location in the white area (200,200 in this case). Add the `setSpeeds` handler to the stack script, below the `startStopCars` handler:

```
on setSpeeds
   put empty into gSpeeds
   repeat with a = 1 to 100
      put "car" & a into carname
      if there is a image carname then
         put (random(10)+10)/10 into item 1 of line a of gSpeeds
         put 0 into item 2 of line a of gSpeeds
         set the loc of image carname to 200,200
      else
```

```
        exit repeat
      end if
   end repeat
end setSpeeds
```

7. In a `moveCars` handler, shown in step 8, we're going to look at the `gBackdropMaskData` variable to see if the car is going to run into something solid. Add this `hitBarrier` function:

```
function hitBarrier pX,pY
    put (pY-1)*gMaskWidth + pX into tStartChar
    put charToNum(char tStartChar of gBackdropMaskData) into
tMaskValue
    if tMaskValue = 255 then return true
    else return false
end hitBarrier
```

8. The `moveCars` handler is initially called by the `startStopCars` handler, and then it will call itself every 2 ticks until the `gMovingCars` variable is set to `false`. Type the long `moveCars` handler into the stack script:

```
on moveCars
    put the long time
    lock screen
    repeat with a = 1 to 100
        put "car" & a into carname
        put .1 into anglechange
        if there is a image carname then
            put 0 into counter
            repeat while counter < 20
                add 1 to counter
                put item 1 of line a of gSpeeds into tCarSpeed
                put item 2 of line a of gSpeeds into tCarDirection
                put item 1 of the loc of image carname into tCarX
                put item 2 of the loc of image carname into tCarY
                put the round of ((cos(tCarDirection)*tCarSpeed)*20 +
                 tCarX) into tLookAheadX
                put the round of ((sin(tCarDirection)*tCarSpeed)*20 +
                 tCarY) into tLookAheadY
                if hitBarrier(tLookAheadX,tLookAheadY) then
                    put tCarDirection + anglechange into item 2 of line
                     a of gSpeeds
                    put anglechange * -1 * ((20 - random(10))/10) into
                     anglechange
                    put max(1,tCarSpeed - .1) into item 1 of line a of
                     gSpeeds
```

```
         else
            put min(3,tCarSpeed + .05) into item 1 of line a of
              gSpeeds
            exit repeat
         end if
      end repeat
      set the loc of image carname to item 1 of the loc of
        image carname + (tLookAheadX-item 1 of the loc of image
          carname)/10,item 2 of the loc of image carname +
            (tLookAheadY-item 2 of the loc of image carname)/10
      set the angle of image carname to 360 - item 2 of line a
        of gSpeeds / PI * 180
    else
       exit repeat
    end if
  end repeat
  unlock screen
  if gMovingCars is true then send moveCars to this card in 2
    ticks
end moveCars
```

Collision avoidance

Take a moment to look at the moveCars handler. What is it doing? You will no doubt have heard about collision detection, this is where you have code that recognizes when one object has collided with another object, or wall perhaps. You might well trigger an explosion, or collision sound when that happens. For our example though we actually don't want things to collide, we want the cars to turn before they would have collided. For each car, up to 100 of them, we look ahead of the car to see if it will collide with the edges of the course. If it's going to do so we change the direction that the car is heading, repeatedly, until a safe forward direction is found.

9. Add a **Start/Stop Cars** button to the card window, and set its script to be:

```
on mouseUp
   startStopCars
end mouseUp
```

10. Select the backdrop image, and choose **Send to Back** from the **Object** menu.

11. Might be a good idea to click on **Save**!

12. Click on the **Run/Browse** tool, and then on the **Start/Stop Cars** button, to see your cars drive around the interface. The following screenshot shows how it looks when 20 cars are moving about:

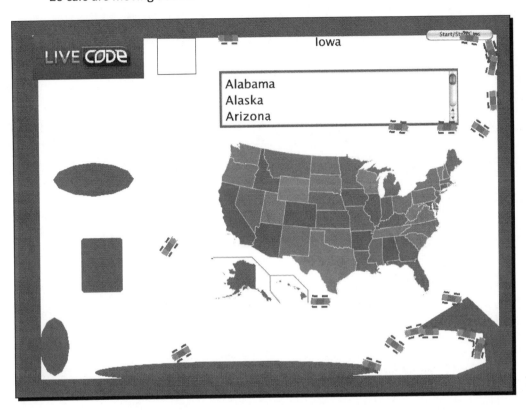

13. Note that you can continue to point to parts of the image you first loaded (the LiveCode logo in the above example), to see the swatch to the right change color. Also, pointing to the different US states should be changing the text in the state field you created.

What just happened?

Having already used `imageData` to implement a color picker, and to act as multiple button areas, we went on to use the `maskData` of the image as a collision map. There is quite a bit of arithmetic behind making the cars move in intelligent ways, and you could go on to change some of the numbers to get different behavior. Or you could take a break, and get ready to make a jigsaw puzzle!

For the US map we only needed to simulate 50 buttons. If you made use of red, green, and blue values, how many buttons could you simulate?

- a. One enormous button.
- b. 65,536 buttons.
- c. 16,777,216 buttons.

Making a jigsaw puzzle

The things we have tried so far in this chapter use techniques that would be useful in any LiveCode application, not specifically with mobile applications. You can try the stack you have constructed; it will work well on a mobile device, even with the color picker, states map, and 20 cars driving around the screen! But those tests didn't really make use of any mobile features. The remainder of the chapter will build on the information about `imageData`, and will also take advantage of a few mobile device features.

Going to pieces...

The general technique we're going to use is to take a set of PNGs that have a nice alpha channel in them (that creates the puzzle piece edges), and then replace the actual pixel data with an image of our own. The first thing we need then is some PNGs.

If you make a commercial mobile application, either create your own puzzle shapes or buy a royalty free image. For prototyping you could grab any image from the web, and get the basics going, then replace the images with higher quality ones that you have bought. Here we are using a preview image from `http://depositphotos.com/` that also sells higher quality versions.

When you do have high quality versions you may wish to create each puzzle piece so that they touch against each other perfectly. Here we're using a preview image, and will select the inner part of each piece, and create the PNGs from those. There will be small gaps between the pieces, but at least it's very quick to prepare the images we'll need.

If you wish to follow along with exactly the same image as shown here, it was taken from the top left-hand side of this file:

```
http://static3.depositphotos.com/1004551/191/v/950/
depositphotos_1914748-Jigsaw-puzzle-blank-templates.jpg
```

1. Make a new **Mainstack** at 1024x768 (or the size of your tablet device). Name the stack `jigsaw`, and set the title to `Jigsaw Puzzle`. Do a Save.

2. Open the whole puzzle image in your image editor.

3. Use the **Magic Wand** tool to pick up the inner part of the upper left-hand side piece of the puzzle.

4. Fill that with a color that makes it easy to spot any remaining gaps.

5. Copy and paste into a new document (with a transparent background) that is the size of the piece you copied.

6. Repair any gaps, using the brush tool set to the same fill color.

7. Save as a PNG (with Photoshop that would be **Save for Web and Devices**, 24 bit, with transparency). Use a naming scheme that will help you identify the images easily. For example, `tlcorner.png`, `p1.png`, `trcorner.png`, and so on.

8. Proceed through all of the differently shaped areas. In the example image that will be as few as 14 unique shapes. There is no need to save other pieces that are the same shape as the ones you already have.

9. The set of images will look like this:

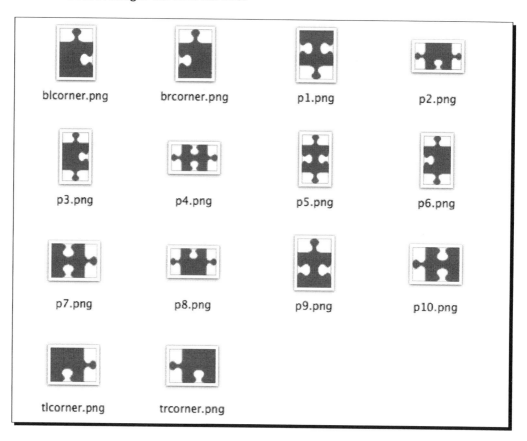

10. In the jigsaw stack, go to **File | Import as Control | Image**, and import all 14 images.

11. Lay out a puzzle that covers most of the card window. In the screens shown below the puzzle was 900x622. Make duplicates of the middle-piece images to fill in the whole puzzle.

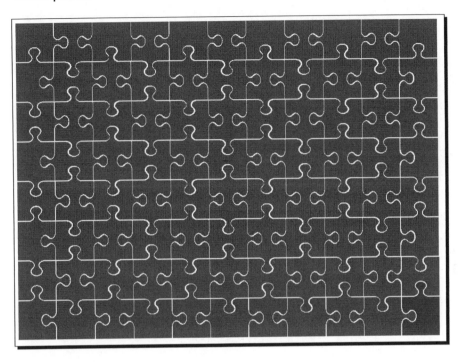

12. Name the images in a grid like fashion. The top left-hand piece would be named p 1 1, the top right-hand side edge piece would be named p 11 1 (there were 11x8 pieces in the 900x662 area), and the bottom right-hand side piece would have a name of p 11 8.

13. Select all of the pieces and Group them. Name the group as pieces.

14. Make a button, with the name of fromcamera and a label of Take a Photo. Set the button scripts to the following:

```
on mouseUp
    loadimage "camera"
end mouseUp
```

15. Make another button, named fromlibrary and labeled Load a Picture, with this script:

```
on mouseUp
    loadimage "library"
end mouseUp
```

16. Edit the card script and add these global variables and functions, which will initialize values that will be needed by the other functions we'll make:

```
global originalimage, puzzlewidth, puzzleheight, snapdistance,
hcount, vcount

on opencard
    setvalues
end opencard

on setvalues
    put 900 into puzzlewidth
    put 662 into puzzleheight
    put 50 into snapdistance
    put 11 into hcount
    put 8 into vcount
end setvalues
```

17. Now add the `loadImage` handler, which the two buttons will call in order to get an image from the user's camera or photo album:

```
on loadImage cameratype
    if puzzlewidth is empty then setvalues
    if there is an image "original" then delete image "original"
    mobilePickPhoto cameratype,puzzlewidth,puzzleheight
    if the result is empty then

        lock screen
        set the name of image the number of images to "original"
        set the width of image "original" to puzzlewidth
        set the height of image "original" to puzzleheight
        put the imageData of image "original" into originalImage
        delete image "original"
        --makepuzzle
        --scatter
        unlock screen
    else
        answer the result
    end if
end loadImage
```

18. The `makepuzzle` and `scatter` lines are commented out for now, so that you can test the functions created so far.

19. Set the buttons to have a drop shadow, using the options in the **Graphic Effects** pane of the **Inspector** palette.

What just happened?

The puzzle pieces are now in place, and named in a way that we can take advantage of when manipulating them. If you go into **Standalone Application Settings** and select **iOS** or **Android**, you can give the app a try.

Setting up some test images.

If you use the iPad Simulator you won't be able to test getting an image from the camera, and at first you won't have any images in the photo library. To solve that, drag images from the **Finder** to the **Simulator** window, and the image will be shown in a **Safari** window. You can then click and hold on the image, and choose **Save Image**. That way you can add a few images to the library in order to select one as the picture for the puzzle.

When LiveCode gets an image from the mobile device, either from the camera or from the library or photo album, it places the picture as an image control that is the topmost object on the card. We don't need the image itself, just its `imageData`, and so in the `loadImage` handler the image is made the same size as the puzzle pieces group, the `imageData` is stored in the global variable `originalImage`, and the image itself is deleted.

Next, we'll transfer the chosen picture into the puzzle pieces.

Time for action – transferring imageData

By setting the chosen image to be the same width and height as the group that holds the puzzle pieces (that's where the 900 and 662 numbers came from), it becomes possible to transfer the matching rectangle of data from the full image to the puzzle piece in question.

1. Open the card script again. Add the **makepuzzle** handler:

```
on makepuzzle
   resetpuzzle
   put the number of images in group "pieces" into imagecount
   repeat with a = 1 to imagecount
      makepiece the short name of image a of group "pieces"
   end repeat
end makepuzzle
```

2. The **makepuzzle** handler will go through each of the puzzle pieces and call another handler to do the transfer of data for that piece. Here is the **makepiece** handler:

```
on makepiece piecename
   put the width of image piecename into piecewidth
   put the height of image piecename into pieceheight
```

```
    put empty into tempimage
    put the left of image piecename - the left of group "pieces"
      into dx
    put the top of image piecename - the top of group "pieces" into
      dy
    repeat with y = 1 to pieceheight
        put ((y+dy-1) * puzzlewidth + dx)*4 into sourcestart
        put char sourcestart+1 to sourcestart+piecewidth*4 of
          originalimage after tempimage
    end repeat
    set the imageData of image piecename to tempimage
end makepiece
```

3. In the earlier `imageData` tests we were only interested in one pixel at a time, but here we want lots of rows of data. The arithmetic, `((y+dy-1) * puzzlewidth + dx)*4 into sourcestart`, quickly pulls out a whole row of pixels at a time. Those rows are built up into a new variable, `tempimage`, which is finally transferred into the actual puzzle piece.

4. After the pieces have their rectangle of the `imageData`, we then need to move the pieces into random places, ready for the user to play the game. That is done with a `scatter` handler:

```
on scatter
    repeat with a = 1 to the number of images in group "pieces"
        set the myloc of image a of group "pieces" to the loc of
image a of group "pieces"
        put the short name of image a of group "pieces" into n
        if edgepiece(n) then
            set the loc of image a of group "pieces" to 40 +
random(400),300 + random(400)
        else
            set the loc of image a of group "pieces" to 500 +
random(500),300 + random(400)
        end if
    end repeat
end scatter
```

5. The first thing that most jigsaw puzzle players do is to separate out the straight-edged pieces. We can code things in a way that saves them a little time, by employing a function that places the edge pieces away from the non-edge pieces. The `edgepiece` function (which is called from the `scatter` handler mentioned earlier) is this:

```
function edgepiece pName
    return word 2 of pName = 1 or word 3 of pName = 1 or word 2 of
pName = hcount or word 3 of pName = vcount
end edgepiece
```

6. The name that we carefully set for each piece is checked to see if that piece is at the left, right, top, or bottom edge of the puzzle. In other words, it's a piece from the outer edge of the puzzle. Scatter places the straight-edged pieces in the left half of the screen, and the others in the right half of the screen.

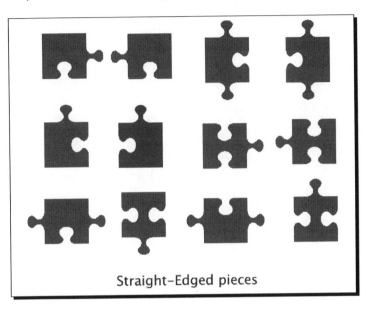

Straight-Edged pieces

7. The start of the `makepuzzle` handler calls a `resetpuzzle` handler. That is used to make sure the pieces are back where they started, ready for a new picture to be loaded. That's achieved by using a property variable on each piece, named `myloc`, which records the initial location. Here's the `resetpuzzle` handler:

```
on resetpuzzle
    repeat with a = 1 to the number of images in group "pieces"
        if the myloc of image a of group "pieces" is not empty then
            set the loc of image a of group "pieces" to the myloc of
              image a of group "pieces"
        else
            set the myloc of image a of group "pieces" to the loc of
              image a of group "pieces"
        end if
    end repeat
end resetpuzzle
```

8. You can see that if `myloc` had not already been set, then the piece must be in its start position, and so the `resetpuzzle` handler goes ahead and records that location in the `myloc` property.

9. Uncomment the lines at step 17 of *Time for Action - creating the pieces and choosing an image* (the `makepuzzle` and `scatter` lines), and try another test of the app. You should now be able to choose a picture and see it as spread out puzzle pieces. Hopefully you will see something like the following screenshot:

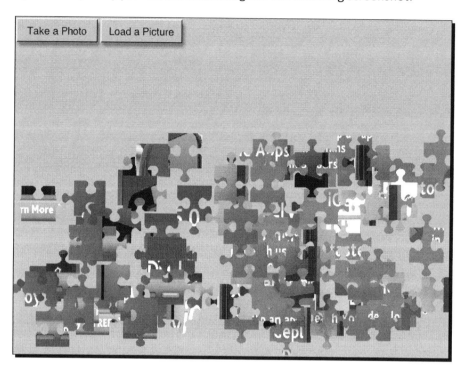

What just happened?

As mentioned above, the right arithmetic made it relatively easy to extract a desired rectangle of `imageData` from a larger image, and to store it in a smaller image the size of that rectangle. But there's one bit of magic that wasn't pointed out; the puzzle kept its shape! How did that happen, seeing as we completely replaced the `imageData` for the image? Setting the `imageData` doesn't interfere with the `alphaData` of the image. The PNGs that we imported kept their original alpha channel, and so still looked the same shape, just with a different image.

Adding interactivity

Our jigsaw puzzle is ready to ship! Well, other than there being no interactivity at all! Let's add some.

Time for action – setting up touch events

The handlers so far have all been in the card script, the plan being to have different cards with different types of puzzle. The interactivity handlers can be placed in the stack script, available to all of the cards.

1. Open the stack script. There is only one global variable that we also need in the stack script, but there are a couple of initializing items to cover. Start the stack script with these lines:

```
global snapdistance

on preopenstack
    if the platform contains "iphone" then
iphoneUseDeviceResolution true
end preopenstack

on openstack
    set the compositorType of this stack to "Static OpenGL"
end openstack
```

2. The `preopenstack` handler checks if the app is on iPhone, and requests that the device's native resolution is used. That will make sure that Retina displays show the best quality. The `compositorType` being set to `Static OpenGL` will help performance.

3. The interactivity we'll use will make use of touch events. Each touch comes with an associated ID value. Here is the handler that detects the start of a touch event:

```
on touchStart touchid
    put the short name of the target into n
    if word 1 of n is "p" then
        set the dropShadow of image n to the dropShadow of button
            "fromlibrary"
        set the relayerGroupedControls to true
        set the layer of the target to the number of images in group
            "pieces"
    end if
end touchstart
```

4. The check of the target name is a quick way to make sure we don't drag anything around except for the puzzle pieces. When a piece is touched we use the `relayerGroupedControls` and `layer` functions to make that piece appear above the other pieces.

5. Do you remember how we added a dropshadow to the two buttons? Aside from making them look nicer, we can make use of it here too. By adding the same dropShadow to the puzzle piece we create the illusion that the piece is floating above the screen.

6. Next thing to watch for is movement, which we can do with the touchMove event:

```
on touchMove touchid,touchx,touchy
    put the short name of the target into n
    if word 1 of n is "p" then
        set the loc of the target to touchx,touchy
    end if
end touchMove
```

7. Again there's a quick double check to make sure it's a puzzle piece, otherwise it's a simple case of setting the location of the piece to the location of the user's finger.

8. When the user releases the piece, we check to see if it's near its starting place, and if it is then we move the piece into place and remove the dropShadow effect:

```
on touchEnd touchid
    put the short name of the target into n
    if word 1 of n is "p" then
        checkdistance the short name of the target
        set the dropShadow of the target to empty
        checkfinished
    end if
end touchEnd
```

9. This is the checkdistance handler, and a distance function it calls:

```
on checkdistance dt
    if snapdistance is empty then put 100 into snapdistance
    put distance(item 1 of the loc of image dt - item 1 of the
     myloc of image dt,item 2 of the loc of image dt - item 2 of
      the myloc of image dt) into d
    if d<snapdistance then
        put max(.1,min(.2,d/200)) into t
        move image dt to the myloc of image dt in t seconds
        set the relayerGroupedControls to true
        set the layer of image dt to 2
    end if
end checkdistance

function distance dx,dy
    return sqrt(dx*dx+dy*dy)
end distance
```

10. The `distance` function uses Pythagoras' formula, returning the number of pixels between the puzzle piece and its original `myloc` value. `snapdistance` is the global variable that is used to determine whether the piece is close enough to its starting place to be considered on target.

11. The `move` line uses LiveCode's `move` function, which will animate the piece into place.

12. One last thing, let's check if the puzzle is completed. Add this handler to the stack script:

```
on checkfinished
    repeat with a = 1 to the number of images in group "pieces"
        if the myloc of image a of group "pieces" <> the loc of
image a of group "pieces" then exit checkfinished
    end repeat
    answer "You've done it!"
end checkfinished
```

What just happened?

The jigsaw puzzle should fully work now. Something that you can't easily guess from the touch functions we added is the fact that it works with multi-touch. You can drag on up to 10 pieces at once (or whatever the multi-touch limit is for your device), and each one will show a drop shadow, and will animate into place when you let go of them.

Have a go hero – one for the kids

Functions that relate to the puzzle itself are in the card script. Try making a new card that has bigger puzzle pieces and a higher value for `snapdistance` (the higher the value, the easier it is to get a piece into place). You could make an opening card for the stack that has a set of difficulty level buttons, one of which would jump to the easier puzzle. That would be ideal for younger players.

Adding some guide graphics will help players know where the edges of the finished puzzle are, and for simpler difficulty levels you might even include outlines of the individual puzzle pieces.

Summary

There are many other possibilities when it comes to making use of `imageData`; in paint programs, image processing applications, and so on. Dealing with the `imageData` is still the same as in the above examples, where we went over the following:

- Understanding the format of `imageData`, `alphaData`, and `maskData`
- Copying areas of `imageData` from one image to another
- Reading individual pixels of an image, and finding novel uses for that value
- We also saw how to use multi-touch interactivity to bring those chunks of `imageData` to life, in the form of a jigsaw puzzle

Working with graphics can be great fun; hopefully this will just be the start of what you will create. However, in the next chapter we'll get back to making a utility application. (Sigh!)

6

Making a Reminder Application

Note to self...

To-do lists, alarms, birthday reminders, notes, shopping lists, the list goes on. There should be an app for keeping a list of different apps that keep the lists! At the time of writing, there were already over 2,000 iPad apps that are lists, planners, or alarms. Perhaps there's room for one more...

It would take a lot of research and money to explore all of the reminders apps that are out there. The majority of the apps will have a lot of features that you'll never use, and at least one vital feature that is missing. If you're lucky, some combination of apps may do all of the things you want. But don't forget, by using LiveCode, you can make your own reminders app!

In this chapter we will:

- ◆ Discuss what is meant by a "reminder"
- ◆ Create some time-measuring utility functions
- ◆ Define a data structure for storing information about an event
- ◆ Make use of mobile device "notifications"
- ◆ Create a flexible reminders app

What is a "reminder"?

Here is a list of few things that you might call a "reminder":

- ◆ Shopping list
- ◆ Christmas present list

◆ To-do list

◆ Alarm clock

◆ Egg timer

◆ Birthday reminder

Now, is there a single way to describe all of those things? Well, it may get wordy, but a reminder could be described as:

A notification message or sound that either appears automatically, or shows when you look for it, which is used to let you know that a certain time has passed, a moment has arrived, or that an outstanding task has not been completed.

See, pretty wordy. Breaking it down like that helps to see what features a reminders app will need to have. Before getting to that, let's test the definition against the examples from here

◆ **Shopping list**: In this case, you go looking for the reminder, although we could set it up to automatically show when your location happens to be near the store! Other than that case, this is effectively a task that has not been completed.

◆ **Christmas present list**: Much the same as a shopping list, but it could use a timed message that let's you know how few shopping days are left.

◆ **To-do list**: Again, it's simply a list of tasks not yet completed.

◆ **Alarm clock**: This is a notification that a moment in time has been reached.

◆ **Egg timer**: This is a notification that a certain amount of time has passed, which could be used in a sequence of such events that might be used in a cooking-buddy app.

◆ **Birthday reminder**: This shows whether a certain moment has been reached. Really though, you want to set the reminder to notify you ahead of the actual event.

At least, as a starting point, we can use the definition to guide us as we outline the abilities the app will need to have.

When?

The mobile notifications that can be created with LiveCode will be sent at the nearest second to when you ask for it to be sent. Strangely though, the value is based on the number of seconds since midnight on January 1st, 1970, specifically in a part of London! Well, it's named after an area of London, called Greenwich.

"Greenwich Mean Time", often referred to as "GMT", has been used as the standard for specifying time. It is now somewhat superseded by UTC (Coordinated Universal Time), but in either case it represents the exact current time, at least for countries that are within the same time zone as Greenwich. The rest of us add or subtract some amount of time to or from that value.

In order to adapt to the fact that the Earth doesn't go around the Sun in an exact number of days, or even an exact number of quarter days, calendars are adjusted by one day every four years, though not on 100 year boundaries, except for every 400 years (2000 was a leap-year for example). Those adjustments are still not enough to keep the clocks on time! The clocks are out of time by about 0.6 seconds a year, and so there are "leap seconds" added to compensate for that. In theory, leap seconds could be used to subtract one second, but as yet this hasn't been needed; they have only been used to add one second.

None of this affects the number of seconds since midnight 1/1/1970, but it does mean that converting LiveCode's seconds into the time and date using your own arithmetic won't give you the right time. And yet it's still used as the basis for notifications. This value is usually referred to as **Unix Time**.

It shouldn't matter much if you end up sending someone a **Happy Birthday** message 25 seconds early! But don't worry, the way we'll calculate the notification time will take care of the oddity.

Date and time pickers

As mentioned previously, mobile notifications use the number of seconds since midnight of 1/1/1970, and don't add on the 25 or so leap seconds that have occurred since then. When we present the date and time pickers to the user, the selections the user makes will come back as the actual current or future time. We will adjust for that later.

Time for action – creating date and time pickers

Make another test-rig stack, which we'll use to try out some date and time pickers.

1. Create a new **Mainstack**, name it `ReminderFunctions`, and save the stack.

2. Add two fields and two buttons.

3. Name one field `dateinseconds` and the other `timeinseconds`.

4. Name the buttons `Pick Date` and `Pick Time`.

5. Set the script of the `Pick Date` button to the following:

```
on mouseUp
   mobilePickDate "date"
   put the result into tDate
   convert tDate to seconds
   put tDate into field "dateinseconds"
end mouseUp
```

6. Set the `Pick Time` button script to this:

```
on mouseUp
   mobilePickDate "time"
   put the result into tTime
   convert tTime to seconds
   put tTime into field "timeinseconds"
end mouseUp
```

7. Set the **Standalone Application Settings**, so that you can test on iOS or Android.

8. Choose your **Test Target** (in this case, you can see that iPhone Simulator was chosen as the target), and do a test.

9. Click on the **Pick Date** button.

10. Select **December 25th, 2012**, and click on **Done**.

11. The number of seconds from midnight 1/1/1970 to midnight of Christmas Day 2012 will be shown in the first field you created.

12. Click on the **Pick Time** button, and set the time to **1 am**. This image shows how the picker looks different on iOS and Android (Kindle Fire in this case):

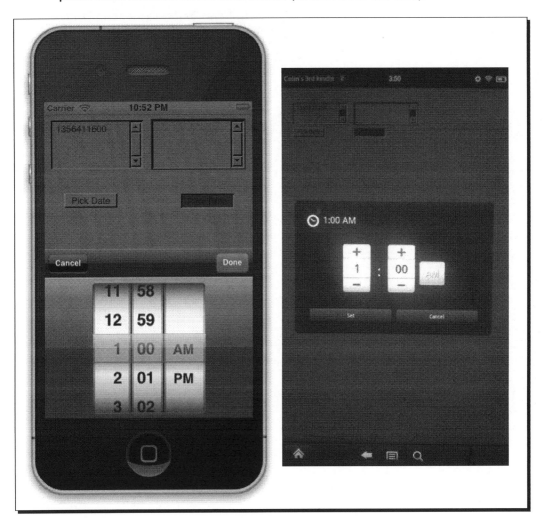

13. Click on **Done**, and you will see the number of seconds from midnight 1/1/1970 to 1am of the day you do this test shown in the right hand field.

What just happened?

We just made two simple scripts that call the native date or time picker, converts the result into seconds, to then show in a field. What is interesting to notice is that for the **Pick Time** case it doesn't return the number of seconds into the current day; it's all of the seconds since midnight 1/1/1970. In order to set a notification time for a particular time of a particular date, we have to do a little arithmetic. We'll go into that a little later, when we make the actual reminder app, in the *Making the reminders app* section of this chapter.

Pop-Quiz – AO (Odd Acronyms!)

1. You may have noticed that the acronym for "Coordinated Universal Time" is UTC and not CUT. Why is that?

    a. CUT is too common a word

    b. So as not to upset the French

    c. The acronym committee members were dyslexic

Where?

There is something we can do in a mobile reminders app that would never work in a pen and paper version; we can present the list of reminders based on where you are at the time that you check! To make use of the location, you need to know where are you now, and how far that is from the place associated with the reminder.

At the time of writing, there is no ability in LiveCode to pull in a map in order for you to choose locations other than the one you are at right now. So, we'll work within that limitation, given that there's no choice!

The general technique when reading mobile device sensors is to start tracking a given sensor, detect when changes happen, and to stop tracking the sensor. You can take a reading from the sensor at any time between the start and stop tracking commands. You can also specify how detailed a report you want, and whether you want a precise reading. The precision for location would dictate whether GPS was used or not. The advantage of using GPS is that you get greater accuracy (assuming there's a clear signal at the time), the disadvantages are that it uses more battery power, and devices that don't have GPS couldn't use that feature. When using location as a part of a reminder, we're mainly interested in whether you're at home, or the office, or perhaps the supermarket. So we'll use the less precise reading, as the GPS one would be overkill.

Time for action – trying out native location tracking

Later we will add in a feature to allow the app user to add to a set of favorite locations. For the moment, we'll just try out the basic functions. Location doesn't work in the simulators; you'll have to try this on a real device.

1. Use the test-rig stack from above, and add a **Get Location** button and a `location` field. Make sure the `location` field is as wide as the card window; it will be showing three long numbers.

2. Set the script of the button to the following:

```
on mouseUp
    mobileStartTrackingSensor "location", true
    put mobileSensorReading("location", false) into field
"location"
    mobileStopTrackingSensor "location"
end mouseUp
```

3. The `true` in the second line is the one that defines a "loose" value, and we're saying that we don't need the precision of GPS. The `false` in the third line is saying that we don't need detailed information to be returned.

4. Go to **Standalone Application Settings**, choose your target device: **iOS** or **Android**.

5. For **iOS**, set **Display Name**, **Internal App ID**, and **Profile**. Choose your device, SDK version, and whether it's to be a Universal app (ARMv6 is for older devices and ARMv7 is for newer devices. For what it's worth, Apple themselves have dropped the support for ARMv6).

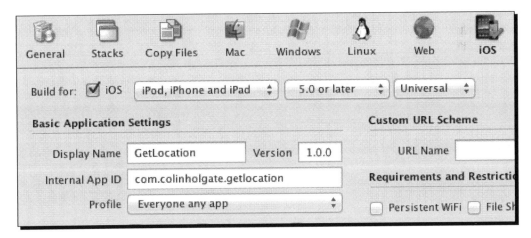

6. For **Android**, set **Label**, **Identifier**, and **Minimum Android Version**.

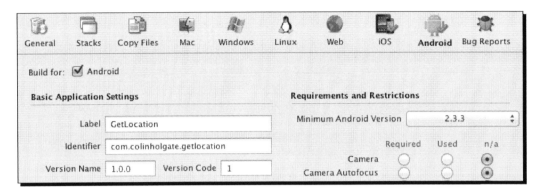

7. Additionally, in the **Application Permissions** part of the Android settings, make sure that you have asked for permission to get **Coarse Location**:

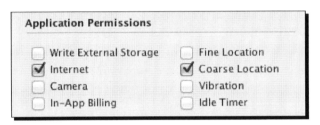

8. Select **Save Standalone Application** and install the app onto your device. Follow the description in *Chapter 2, Getting Started with LiveCode Mobile*, if you need a reminder on how to do that!

9. In the app, try the **Pick Date** and **Pick Time** buttons to see how they bring up the native controls, and then touch the **Get Location** button. Three long numbers should appear in the location field:

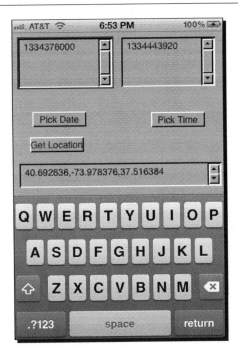

What just happened?

As you can see, there is very little code needed to read a location! If this was a tracking app, then you would need to keep the tracking open and have functions to respond to the change of location messages. But, for our app, we just need to know where you are at the time you take a look at your list of reminders.

The numbers that are shown in the location field are the **latitude**, **longitude**, and **elevation** of the position of the device. But how will we use those numbers...

Calculating the distance between two points on Earth

The plan is to be able to sort your reminders list in order of distance from where you are right now. Let's say you really use this app a lot and have dozens of reminders. The reminder you created about buying some bread may be at the bottom of the list, but if you have assigned the location of the supermarket to that reminder, then sorting the list while you're outside the supermarket should bring the shopping list items to the top.

When faced with a problem such as this one - how to find the distance between two points on Earth - Google is a good starting place! It takes very little searching time to find this page:

```
http://www.movable-type.co.uk/scripts/latlong.html
```

The article there discusses the original formula for doing this calculation, and then shows a Javascript function. If you find it hard to convert the equation into LiveCode handlers, then you ought to be able to convert the Javascript, line by line, into the LiveCode equivalent.

No need to type this in just yet; we'll integrate it later. But if you want to have a play, put these lines into the stack script:

```
function distance lat1,lon1,lat2,lon2
    put 6371 into r
    put toRad((lat2-lat1)) into dLat
    put toRad((lon2-lon1)) into dLon
    put toRad(lat1) into lat1
    put toRad(lat2) into lat2
    put sin(dLat.2) * sin(dLat/2) + sin(dLon/2)*sin(dLon/2) *
cos(lat1)*cos(lat2) into a
    put 2*atan2(sqrt(a),sqrt(1-a)) into c
    put r*c into d
    return d
end distance

function toRad pAngle
    return pAngle/180*PI
end toRad
```

Try this in the message box:

```
put distance(40,-74,51,0)
```

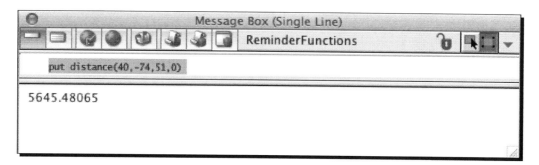

As shown, you should see a value of **5645.48065**. The two locations are somewhere near New York and London, and that value would be the distance in kilometers between the two, traveling along the surface of the Earth.

1. Examine the earlier screenshot (the one timed at **6:53PM**), and given the clue that the building I live in is not much above sea level, which floor do I live on?

    a. 40th floor

    b. 73 floors below ground

    c. 11th floor

    d. I'm homeless

What?

We're well on the way to knowing how to set a time and date for the reminder notification to occur, and will be able to sort the reminders based on the distance from where we are. But what exact information do we need to have in the reminder itself?

If this were a birthday reminder app, then you would just need to ask for the person's name and the date for their birthday. If it were a shopping list app, then you would need the name of the item and maybe a quantity. For a timer, you would need to ask what the event was called and a time for the event.

Here though, we're trying to make a completely flexible reminder app; it would be up to the user to describe the item however they like. So we'll just ask for a title and a brief description. We will also need to offer the option of setting a date, a time, an associated location, and whether an alert sound should be played or not.

Another thing to think about is where will we store the information for the list of reminders? When doing the WebScraper app, we chose to duplicate the main application stack into the documents folder, and to then jump into that copy of the stack. This enabled the ability to save the changes to the stack. The reminders app is a simpler case; we're only trying to store a few text strings to define each reminder, and it would be simpler to just write a text file.

We want to allow the user to make a list of locations, so that a reminder can be associated with that location. Rather than writing a different text file, we will make the first piece of information in each entry be the function of that entry. Right now, the only two functions are location and reminder. Here is an example of what the text file might look like:

```
Location    Home   40.692636    -73.978376
Location    Office 40.745194    -73.985199
Reminder    Packt  Ask for more time!  1334548800    Home    false
Reminder    Boss   Buy lunch    1334592000    Office true
```

Between each item in a line is a tab character, which will be used for separating the parts of the entry. The structure for a Location is as follows:

- Function – "Location"
- Location's title
- Latitude
- Longitude

For a Reminder, it's as follows:

- Function – "Reminder"
- Title
- Brief description
- Notification time, in seconds since midnight 1/1/1970
- A Location associated with this reminder
- Whether to play an alert sound ("true" or "false")

Making the reminders app

Ok, enough groundwork! Let's start to make the reminders app. Rather than adding a feature at a time along with any scripts, we'll make the various cards that will be needed to create the app's **Graphical User Interface (GUI)** first, and then go back and add the scripts.

Laying out the cards

We're going to make the first card of the stack be a place where you can see the current reminders, sort them by time or location, and add new reminders and locations. Then, we will make a second card for entering the location details, and a third card for entering details for a new reminder.

Time for action – creating the reminder app screens

The steps shown here are going to use the standard LiveCode fields and buttons, but feel free to make your version more attractive!

1. Create a new **Mainstack**, give it a name of `EasyReminder`, and select **Save**. Other options such as `Simple Reminders` might be more descriptive, but would be too long a name if you're using an iPhone.

2. Set the card size to the size of your device. The screenshots shown next are based on an iPhone sized stack.

3. Go into **Standalone Application Settings**, and set the values in the same way that we did while testing the Location feature.

4. Set the name of the first card to be home.

5. Create a Sort by Time **button, a** Sort by Location **button, one field named** reminders, **another field named** data, **and two buttons named** Create Reminder... **and** Create Location....

6. Add one more button, named Delete Location or Reminder.

7. Make sure that both fields have their **Lock** text box checked, and **Don't wrap** checked.

8. You should have something similar to the following:

9. Make a new card and name it `location`.

10. Add a field, and set its contents to say: `Enter the latitude and longitude for this location`.

11. Add two input fields named `latitude` and `longitude`.

12. Create a button named `Set to Current Location`.

Avoid typos

Although we have placed a field for you to type in the location by hand, use the **Set to Current Location** button if possible, or at least use that at your current location to see the format that is required.

13. Add another instructions field that says: `Enter a name for this location:`.

14. Add a third input field, named `location name`.

15. Finally, add a button named `Add Location` and one named `Cancel`.

16. For this card, all three fields need their **Lock text** box to be unchecked.

17. The card should be similar to the following:

18. Make a third card and name it `reminder`.

19. Add two instruction fields that say: `Enter a title for this reminder:` and `Enter a brief description:`.

20. Create two more input fields named `title` and `description`.

21. Create three buttons named `Set Related Location`, `Set Date`, and `Set Time`.

22. Add three fields next to those buttons, which will be used to show the user that the selection they made took place. Name the fields `location field`, `date field`, and `time field`.

23. Create a checkbox button named `Play Alert Sound`.

24. Lastly, create two more buttons named `Add Reminder` and `Cancel`.

25. Arrange all of these elements to appear as follows:

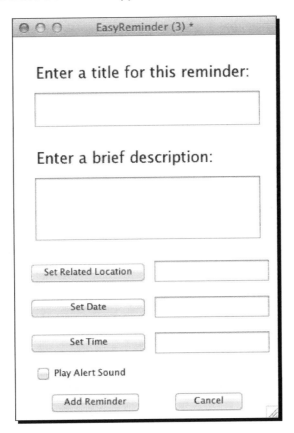

What just happened?

We've made all of the screens needed for the app to function. That was the easy bit. Just wait until you see how much typing you are going to do!

Stack level scripts

There is quite a bit of code ahead. Describing it feature by feature would involve jumping all over the place, adding to existing scripts in some cases, and it would be easy to get lost. So instead of doing it that way we'll look at the code for each card at a time, and also at the handlers that go into the Stack script. It's shown here in "Time for action" chunks, mainly to give you a break now and then! So without further ado, the Stack script...

Time for action – adding Stack level functions

For this app, we're going to put some of the logic in the buttons on the cards themselves, but it still leaves a good amount that goes into the Stack script. To make it less overwhelming, we'll show one or two functions at a time followed by some explanation about any interesting points.

1. Open the Stack script.

2. Type in the following handlers:

```
on openstack
    if the platform is "iphone" then iPhoneSetKeyboardReturnKey
"done"
    readdata
    showdata
end openstack

on returnInField
    focus on nothing
end returnInField
```

> Android OS keyboards generally have a button dedicated to putting the keyboard away. However, that isn't the case on iOS; the button that sits where the *Return* key should be may have a special word instead, such as **Send**, or **Done**. Unfortunately, we are entering text into fields that are able to take a return character. To solve this issue, we set the *Return* button to say **Done**, which will lead the user to expect the keyboard to go away when that button is pressed. We will also trap the `returnInField` message, and use that as a way to actually put the keyboard away.

3. Next, type in the functions that will read and write the list of reminders as a text file to the documents folder on your device:

```
on writedata
    global gReminderData
    put specialFolderPath("documents") & "/reminders.txt" into
tRemindersPath
    if gReminderData is empty then put "no entries yet" into
gReminderData
    open file tRemindersPath
    write gReminderData to file tRemindersPath
    close file tRemindersPath
    clearnotifiers
    setupnotifiers
end writedata

on readdata
    global gReminderData
    put specialFolderPath("documents") & "/reminders.txt" into
tRemindersPath
    if there is a file tRemindersPath then
        open file tRemindersPath
        read from file tRemindersPath until eof
        close file tRemindersPath
        put it into gReminderData
    else
        open file tRemindersPath
        write "no entries yet" to file tRemindersPath
        close file tRemindersPath
        put "no entries yet" into gReminderData
    end if
end readdata
```

 These two functions are using the straightforward ability that LiveCode has to read and write text files. Notice though that specialFolderPath is being used to help work out where the file will be saved. It even works when testing on desktop machines. The LiveCode dictionary shows a full list of special folder paths, including many that don't apply to mobile apps.

4. The showdata function could well have been put into the Home card's Card script, but having it in the Stack level keeps it near other functions that are related. Type it in now.

```
on showdata
    global gReminderData
```

```
go card "home"
put empty into field "reminders"
put gReminderData into field "data"
if gReminderData = "no entries yet" then
   exit showdata
end if
set the itemdelimiter to tab
put 1 into tLineNumber
repeat with a = 1 to the number of lines in gReminderData
    put line a of gReminderData into tEntry
    if item 1 of tEntry = "Reminder" then
        put item 2 of tEntry into tTitle
        put item 3 of tEntry into tDescription
        put item 4 of tEntry into tNotificationTime
        convert tNotificationTime from seconds to abbreviated
time and long date
        put item 5 of tEntry into tLocationName
        put tTitle & ":" && tDescription && tNotificationTime &&
tLocationName into line tLineNumber of field "reminders"
        add 1 to tLineNumber
    end if
  end repeat
end showdata
```

If you recall the sample text file from earlier, the showdata function is taking each line and splitting the tab delimited items into chunks of information to present to the user. One cute trick is that the notification time, which is a long number of seconds, is converted into a human readable form, showing both the date and time of the notification. The data field is being used to show the raw data that has been saved. In the final application you would not show this, but it's handy for checking whether the reminder information looks correct.

5. The last functions in the Stack script are for setting up the notifications themselves.

```
on clearnotifiers
   mobileCancelAllLocalNotifications
end clearnotifiers

on setupnotifiers
   global gReminderData
   if gReminderData = "no entries yet" then exit setupnotifiers
   set the itemdelimiter to tab
   repeat with a = 1 to the number of lines in gReminderData
      put line a of gReminderData into tEntryDetails
```

```
        if item 1 of tEntryDetails = "Reminder" then
            put item 2 of tEntryDetails && "-" && item 3 of
tEntryDetails into alertBody
            put "OK" into alertButtonMessage
            put tEntryDetails into alertPayload
            put item 4 of tEntryDetails into alertTime
            put item 6 of tEntryDetails into playSound
            mobileCreateLocalNotification alertBody,
alertButtonMessage, alertPayload, alertTime, playSound
        end if
    end repeat
end setupnotifiers

on localNotificationReceived pMsg
    answer "Local Notification:" && pMsg
end localNotificationReceived
```

Many mobile apps that use notifications don't ever clear them. In general, maybe they don't need to be cleared, once they go by they're gone for good! Well, not always. Sometimes you'll go into an app just ahead of when a notification is going to happen, and you do the task, only to then be pestered with notifications about something you already did! In our app, we clear all notifications that were due and recreate the whole list again. This way, any notifications that you have deleted won't come back to haunt you later. To help in debugging, alertPayload is filled in with the entire reminder entry, and will be shown to you when the notification comes in.

What just happened?

In addition to getting your fingers nicely warmed up, you entered all of the functions for reading and writing the reminder data, and for creating and receiving the notification messages.

Home card scripts

We're not going to put any scripts into the card level; they can just be inside the various buttons, starting with the ones on the first card.

Time for action – making the Home card buttons work

The **Sort by Location** button's script is quite something. You should look forward to that! But first, we'll start with the **Sort by Time** button.

1. Edit the script of the **Sort by Time** button, on the first card.

2. Type in this short handler:

```
on mouseUp
   global gReminderData
   set the itemdelimiter to tab
   sort gReminderData numeric by item 4 of each
   showdata
   writedata
end mouseUp
```

> LiveCode's sort command is powerful, and in the above case, it is sorting the list of reminders based on the notification seconds value. Once the lines are sorted, the list for the user to see is recreated, and the text file is rewritten.

3. Get mentally prepared and then edit the script of the **Sort by Location** button.

4. Type in all of this:

```
on mouseUp
   global gReminderData
   mobileStartTrackingSensor "location", true
   put mobileSensorReading("location", false) into tLocation
   mobileStopTrackingSensor "location"
   set the itemdelimiter to comma
   put item 1 of tLocation into tLat
   put item 2 of tLocation into tLong
   set the itemdelimiter to tab
   sort gReminderData numeric by getdistance(tLat,tLong,item 5 of
each)
   showdata
   writedata
end mouseUp

function getdistance pLat,pLong,pLocName
   if pLocName is empty then return 1000000
   global gReminderData
   put empty into tLat
```

```
    put empty into tLong
    repeat with a = 1 to the number of lines in gReminderData
        if item 1 of tEntryDetails = "Location" then
            if item 2 of tEntryDetails = pLocName then
                put item 3 of tEntryDetails into tLat
                put item 4 of tEntryDetails into tLong
            end if
        end if
    end repeat
    if tLat is empty then return 1000000000
    return distance(tLat,tLong,pLat,pLong)
end getdistance

function distance lat1,lon1,lat2,lon2
    put 6371 into r
    put toRad((lat2-lat1)) into dLat
    put toRad((lon2-lon1)) into dLon
    put toRad(lat1) into lat1
    put toRad(lat2) into lat2
    put sin(dLat/2) * sin(dLat/2) + sin(dLon/2)*sin(dLon/2) *
cos(lat1)*cos(lat2) into a
    put 2*atan2(sqrt(a),sqrt(1-a)) into c
    put r*c into d
    return d
end distance

function toRad pAngle
    return pAngle/180*PI
end toRad
```

The first part of the `mouseUp` handler is just getting your current location. The `distance` and `toRad` functions are the same ones we looked at earlier. The magic happens in the way that the sort line uses a function to determine the sort order. By passing the location that you associated with each reminder into the `getdistance` function, it's possible to run through the list of locations to find a match, and then use that location's latitude and longitude to measure the distance from your current location. That distance is then used by the sort command in deciding the order of the lines.

5. For a moment's relaxation, edit the **Create Reminder...** button script, and set it to the following:

```
on mouseUp
    go to card "reminder"
end mouseUp
```

6. Likewise, set the "Create Location..." button script to this:

```
on mouseUp
    go to card "location"
end mouseUp
```

7. Last script for this card, edit the **Delete Location or Reminder** button script, and type in this:

```
on mouseUp
    global gReminderData
    mobilePick gReminderData,1,"checkmark","cancelDone","picker"
    put the result into tItemsToDelete
    if tItemsToDelete = "0" then exit mouseUp
    set the itemdelimiter to comma
    repeat with a = the number of items in tItemsToDelete down to 1
        delete line (item a of tItemsToDelete) of gReminderData
    end repeat
    if gReminderData is empty then put "no entries yet" into
gReminderData
    showdata
    writedata
end mouseUp
```

> The `delete` handler uses `mobilePick` with a particular set of parameters. One interesting parameter is `checkmark`. Asking for that type of picker will show a list with checkboxes in it when you're on iPad or Android. This would enable you to choose several entries to delete in one go. Hence `repeat` the loop that goes through as many items as you chose.

What just happened?

All being well, you have recovered by now after trying to understand the sort by location function! You can see at least how tough the Stack script would have been if all of this code had been placed in that one location. Let's go on to the next card...

Creating a location card

Next up is the card that we will show when the user touches the **Create a Location...** button on the first card.

Time for action – making the location card work

The Location card has three fields in it, for latitude, longitude, and a title for the location. The user could well type in the details manually, but if they happen to be at the location in question there's a button there to grab the location and to fill in the numbers automatically.

1. Edit the script of the **Set to Current Location** button, and type in the following lines:

```
on mouseUp
    mobileStartTrackingSensor "location", true
    put mobileSensorReading("location", false) into tLocation
    mobileStopTrackingSensor "location"
    set the itemdelimiter to comma
    if the number of items in tLocation = 3 then
        put item 1 of tLocation into field "latitude"
        put item 2 of tLocation into field "longitude"
    end if
end mouseUp
```

2. Nothing too tricky there, the location is grabbed and the latitude and longitude entries are stored in the two fields.

3. Edit the script of the **Cancel** button, and change it to this easy script:

```
on mouseUp
    go to card "home"
end mouseUp
```

4. Last item for this card; edit the **Add Location** button script, and type in the following:

```
on mouseUp
    global gReminderData
    if field "location name" is empty then
        answer "Please enter a name for this location."
        exit mouseUp
    end if
    if field "latitude" is empty or field "longitude" is empty then
        answer "Please enter location values, or press the 'Set to
Current Location' button."
        exit mouseUp
    end if
    put "Location" & tab & field "location name" & tab & field
"latitude" & tab & field "longitude" into tLocationDetails
    if gReminderData = "no entries yet" then
        put tLocationDetails into gReminderData
    else
```

```
            put return & tLocationDetails after gReminderData
        end if
        go to card "home"
        showdata
        writedata
    end mouseUp
```

5. Most of that handler is just checking to see that the user entered the required information.

What just happened?

A lot less happened than on the first card! But it was equally important. Now we have a way for the user to set up a location to be used by the reminders they have created. And that's where we're heading now...

Reminder entry form

This last card is essentially an entry form; we just want to ask the user what the reminder is for. There are some tricky aspects to it though, and one or two lengthy functions to cope with that.

Time for action – taking in information about the reminder

The Reminder card makes good use of pickers. There is little typing for the user to do, and because they will pick an entry from a list that we present, there's a good chance the information won't have any typos in it!

1. Edit the script of the **Set Related Location** button, and type in the following:

```
on mouseUp
    global gReminderData
    put empty into tLocations
    set the itemdelimiter to tab
    put 1 into tLineNumber
    repeat with a = 1 to the number of lines in gReminderData
        if item 1 of line a of gReminderData = "Location" then
            put item 2 to 4 of line a of gReminderData into line
tLineNumber of tLocations
            add 1 to tLineNumber
        end if
    end repeat
    if tLocations is empty then
        answer "You need to add a location."
```

```
    else
        mobilePick tLocations,1
        put the result into tChosenLocation
        if tChosenLocation >0 then
            put item 1 of line tChosenLocation of tLocations into
field "location field"
        end if
    end if
end mouseUp
```

> We set the first word of each line in the reminders data to either
> Location or Reminder. Here's one place where we make
> use of that. Once we pull out the lines that are Location,
> presenting them inside a picker is easy to do.

2. Edit the script of the **Set Date** button, and change it to this easy-to-understand script:

```
on mouseUp
    mobilePickDate "date"
    put the result into tDate
    convert tDate to seconds
    put tDate into field "date field"
end mouseUp
```

3. Set the script of the **Set Time** button to this almost identical script:

```
on mouseUp
    mobilePickDate "time"
    put the result into tTime
    convert tTime to seconds
    put tTime into field "time field"
end mouseUp
```

4. The **Cancel** button script is the same as it is on the Location card:

```
on mouseUp
    go to card "home"
end mouseUp
```

5. Last, and far from least, the **Add Reminder** button script does all the hard work.

```
on mouseUp
    global gReminderData
    if field "title" is empty or field "description" is empty then
        answer "Please enter both a title and a description."
        exit mouseUp
```

```
      end if
      put "false" into tDoAlert
      if the hilite of button "Play Alert Sound" then put "true" into
   tDoAlert
      put field "date field" into tDateValue
      put field "time field" into tTimeValue
      convert tTimeValue from seconds to short date
      convert tTimeValue to seconds
      put field "time field" - tTimeValue into tTimeValue
      add tTimeValue to tDateValue
      put "Reminder" & tab & field "title" & tab & field
   "description" into tReminderDetails
      put tReminderDetails & tab & tDateValue & tab & field "location
   field" & tab into tReminderDetails
      put tReminderDetails & tab & tDoAlert into tReminderDetails
      if gReminderData = "no entries yet" then
         put tReminderDetails into gReminderData
      else
         put return & tReminderDetails after gReminderData
      end if
      go to card "home"
      showdata
      writedata
   end mouseUp
```

Most of the above script is just combining the different bits of information together into one reminder entry, delimiting the parts with a tab character. But there is one bit of cute arithmetic going on in there too. At the start of this chapter, we looked at how Unix Time differs from actual time at a rate of 0.6 seconds per year. If you want to set a notification to be 8 a.m. in five years from now, then you can't take the value that the **Set Time** button gave you, because that refers to today's 8 a.m.. You can't take the value that **Set Date** gave you, because that would be midnight. So, by converting the time value into short date format, and then back to seconds format, you find out what the Unix Time was at midnight of the current day. Subtracting that from the value that **Set Time** gave you lets you know the number of seconds since midnight, regardless of how many seconds behind Unix Time is. Adding that value to the one from **Set Date** will give us an exact Unix Time seconds for the notification to occur. Under iOS, there is a picker type that allows you to set the date and the time together, but as that isn't on Android, we've used a way that works for both.

What just happened?

Phew! We got to the end! Try to run the app on your device. If your fingers aren't too numb that is! Honestly, you could bet a fortune that it won't work the first time, but if it works well enough to show the raw text in the data field on the first card, hopefully you'll be able to track down any errors in the code. You can also type in some test data into the stack on your computer and at least test the functions that don't require device-specific features.

Have a go hero – nice transitions

Really, if you managed to get through entering all that code to the point where the app is working, you're already a hero! However, read the section in the iOS and Android release notes for LiveCode about *Visual effects support*. See if you can get some typical mobile OS transitions happening as you go to and from the different cards. If you chose to use MobGUI as a way to make the app look prettier, then take a look in its default button scripts; there are commented-out lines that will get you started with doing nice transitions.

Summary

This chapter was way more exciting than expected! A reminders app is absolutely not quite as impressive as Angry Birds, but, making use of the location features of a mobile device made it a little more novel. Along the way we dabbled with these things:

◆ Reading and writing data to the special documents folder

◆ Use of pickers for straightforward lists, dates, and time

◆ Reading the current location of the device

◆ Setting up of local notification events

In the best of cases, you can manage to make a mobile app in a few hours or days, but there is quite a lot that goes on before you can submit the app to the various app stores. Sounds like a good topic for the next chapter!

7

Deploying to Your Device

Don't keep it all to yourself!

Tools such as LiveCode can be used entirely for personal productivity applications, and would more than pay for themselves in the time that it would save you every day. But why not let the rest of the world benefit from your creations!

So far we have created several little test-rig apps, and a few more fleshed out ones. In all cases though, we've just tested those inside simulators or on your own personal device. The time has come to get it out to more people, for beta testing at first, and then for uploading to the different app stores.

In this chapter we will cover the following:

- Examine all the **Standalone Application Settings** options that relate to creating mobile apps
- Create builds of an app so that it can be sent to beta testers
- Build a final distribution version of an app
- Review how to upload apps to the iOS App Store, Amazon AppStore, and Google Play

There are some stages in creating iOS apps for the App Store that have to be performed on a Mac, and so all of the iOS steps described here should be followed using a Mac. The Android steps can apply to Mac or Windows. Note too that this chapter is more of a reference, and not a hands-on walkthrough. When you have an app that is getting ready for completion and submission to app stores, and you hit a sticking point, hopefully you will recall reading about the issue somewhere in this chapter!

Standalone Application Settings

You have already been into the settings a few times by now, but we've only made the minimum number of changes needed in order to test the app. There are a lot of options in there that you will need to fill in before your app is ready to be sold in an app store. We'll briefly go over the other standalone application sections, and then go into more depth with the Android and iOS sections.

General

The **General** section of the standalone settings is used primarily for controlling which features of LiveCode are to be included in a desktop standalone application. Those options don't apply to mobile applications, but it is in the **General** section that you set the name of the application file, and also the build folder (those items of interest are at the top and bottom of the dialog box):

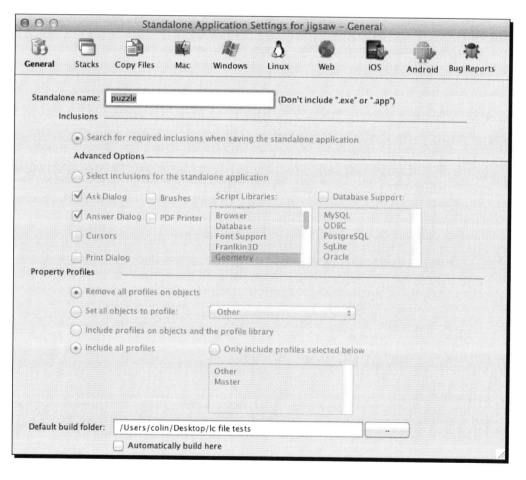

Stacks

The **Stacks** section will show you a list of the stacks that are already included in your project. That will of course include the current **Mainstack**, and will also include stacks that have been added by plugins such as **MobGui**. All the options will be grayed out.

Copy Files

The **Copy Files** section is used for adding the additional files and folders to be used by your app. These are going to be read-only files, if you need changeable files you could still include those files here, and then write copies of the files to the special documents folder. Here is how the dialog box looks with folders of images and sounds added:

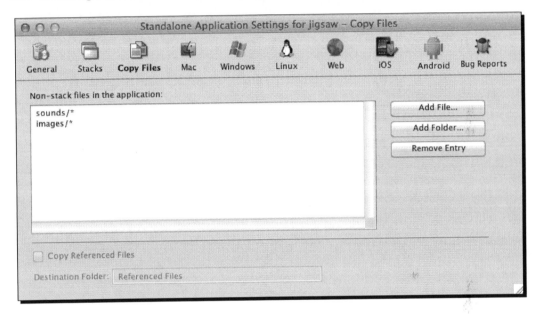

iOS

The **Mac**, **Windows**, **Linux**, **Web**, and **Bug Reports** sections are not used when making iOS and Android apps, so now we'll take a good look at the **iOS** section, bit by bit...

Build for

The **Build for** settings determine which iOS devices the app will work on, and what the minimum iOS version needs to be. In deciding what to choose, some things are obvious while others are not so obvious. If you are making an app that really needs a large area of workspace, then it might not be too successful on an iPod or iPhone screen. If it's a small utility that is geared towards use on a hand-held device, perhaps you don't need to have an iPad version. You are able to choose **iPod**, **iPhone**, and **iPad**, or just **iPod and iPhone**, and even just **iPad**.

The minimum iOS version you choose may depend on particular features you have used. You don't want users to be allowed to buy your app only to find that a certain feature doesn't work correctly under their older iOS version. You may need to keep some devices, set to use old versions of the OS, for testing so that you can be sure whether your setting is correct. Also, Xcode allows you to download various versions of the Simulator, and in LiveCode you can choose a specific version to test against.

The last selection is the processor used on the device. Your choices are **Universal**, **Arm v6**, and **Arm v7**. These refer to instruction sets used in mobile processors. On iOS, things are more straightforward than on Android, in that the processors are referred to as **Armv6** or **Armv7**. With Android there are many more processor types, and it can take a bit of research to find out which instruction set is used for a given processor.

Apple themselves have dropped support for ARMv6. iOS version 4.3 and later requires ARMv7. The devices that are ARMv7 are the iPhones since the 3GS, and the iPod Touch since the 3rd generation, except for the 8GB version of the 3rd generation, which was still ARMv6. You may have an app that works well even on the original iPhone, but if you are in any doubt about how it will perform, choosing **Arm v7** may be a good idea. You could also choose a minimum iOS version of **4.3 or later**, or even **5.0 or later**. Some web browser features worked better after iOS version 5.0 was released.

You can always leave these options set to lower values for now, and make up your mind after you have heard how your beta testers got on with the app.

Here is the **Build for** area of the settings, along with the menus you can choose from:

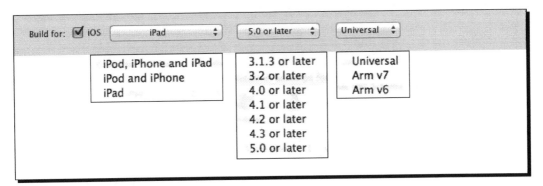

Basic Application Settings

We have used some of these settings a few times already. Here is the full set of options:

- ◆ **Display Name**: the name that will appear under the icon on the actual device
- ◆ **Version**: the version number that will appear in the iTunes description for the app
- ◆ **Internal App ID**: the app ID that you used in the iOS Developer Portal when making the development or distribution provisioning profile
- ◆ **Profile**: the provisioning profile that matches this app
- ◆ **Externals**: a set of optional external command files that you may have used in your app

You should try out different display names to see how it looks on devices. There is a limit to how long the name can be before iOS truncates the name, placing ellipses in the middle of the text. For iPhone that is roughly 11 or 12 characters.

It's important to make sure that an update to an app that you submit should have a version number that is later than the existing app. Starting with 1.0.0 makes sense, just remember to increase the number when you do your updates. Don't worry, if you forget you'll find the upload process to the App Store will fail! App stores in general require that the update be a later version than the one that is being replaced.

For development purposes you can use a provisioning profile that uses an internal app ID that contains a wildcard. When you do submit an app to the iOS App Store, make sure that the provisioning profile is a Distribution one, and that the App ID it uses exactly matches the **Internal App ID**. Also, make sure the ID is different to any other app that you have in the store. Note though that the ID as shown in your developer account page will show extra digits at the start of the ID, for example: `31415926.com.yourname.yourappname`. The matching **Internal App ID** would be `com.yourname.yourappname`.

In the following example screenshot, a development provisioning file is chosen, and also no external commands were used:

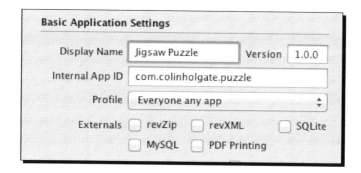

Icons

You are able to select a different icon for each type that iOS and iTunes require. The **Icons** area is straightforward; you click on the **...** button and choose the file from your file system. It would be possible for LiveCode to take one large image and to create the various sizes for you, but there isn't an option for that! For what it's worth, you may have reasons to show a different icon for each case. For example, you could make an icon for Retina displays that had more detail in it than could be seen on a non-Retina display. As you don't have a choice, just enjoy the flexibility this gives you!

Note the **Prerendered Icon** checkbox. You have a choice of creating an icon exactly as it should appear on devices. Or, you could produce a square icon with no shading, and leave the system to make it look like a button with a highlight effect. Take a look at the various apps on your own devices; you will find that some people were happy to use Apple's beveled highlighted appearance, and others preferred to do their own thing. The **Prerendered Icon** feature allows you to do your own thing. In this screenshot you can see that icons for all types have been selected, even iPad Retina, and they are not pre-rendered:

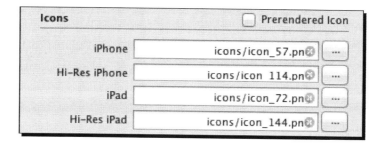

Splash Screens

Since the very first iPhone, iOS has had the ability to load and show a splash screen immediately when a user touches an app icon. This gives them something to look at while the app is loading. All that was needed in those days was a default image, and it had a name of `Default.png`. When the iPad came along there was now a need for more splash screens. At the very least you needed a higher resolution default image, but also you needed custom images for landscape, even going so far as to having different landscape images depending on whether the home button is to the left-hand side or right-hand side.

LiveCode doesn't give access to that level of flexibility, but it is extremely rare that an app would need a different landscape for the two variations; you can generally get by with just the one. Same for the upside-down portrait variation; the regular default portrait image can be used for that too.

The Retina displays have their own entries for setting the splash screen, and by convention those files would have names that include an `@2x` part to the name.

Which of the splash screen options are enabled is dependent on the orientation options, as described in the next section. In this screenshot, the **iPad Portrait** options are grayed out, because the app is set to be landscape only:

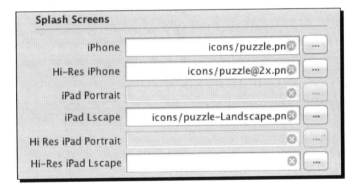

You may notice that there isn't an iPhone portrait or landscape option. That's because the `Default.png` is used for both. If your app is landscape only, then design the splash screen as landscape, but rotate the image 90 degrees clockwise to create a 320x480 or 640x960 `Default.png` or `Default@2x.png` image.

Orientation Options

As discussed above, you are able to specify what orientations are supported by your app. If the app is just for iPod and iPhone, you can only set what the initial orientation is. The choices are **Portrait**, **Portrait Upside-Down**, **Landscape Left**, and **Landscape Right**. If it is for iPad, then you can also set which orientations are supported while the app is in use. The selections you make will affect what icons can be imported. The orientations are all set with just one drop-down menu and four checkboxes:

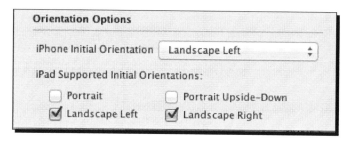

Custom URL Scheme

Sometimes when using an iOS device you will touch a URL in a web page, and suddenly you will find yourself in Mail, or looking at a page in the App Store. This is achieved by using a **Custom URL Scheme**. In the case of the App Store, links begin with **itms-apps://**, and from that iOS knows that the link should be opened in the App Store app. You can do the same thing with your app. By setting a similar custom string you can then get iOS to open your app when the user touches a link that starts with the same string in the URL. The value of the string is entered with a simple text input field as shown in the following screenshot:

Requirements and Restrictions

Earlier we talked about how setting the device, processor instruction set, and iOS version, is one way to make sure that your users are able to use the features in your app. The **Requirements and Restrictions** options let you specify in great detail what abilities the device should have. At the very least, if you have an app that involves taking photographs, requiring a camera could be a good idea! If it's a video chat app, requiring a front camera would make sense. The reminders app that we made in the previous chapter should have its **Location Services** option selected, to make sure that the sort by distance feature would work. Here's the full list:

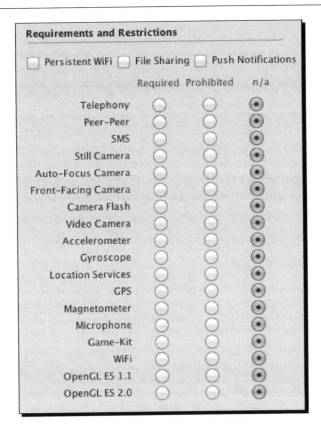

Status Bar

The last option in the iOS settings controls whether the status bar is to be visible or not, and whether it should have the default status bar appearance, or a black appearance. For the black appearance you can set whether it is to be opaque or translucent. The following screenshot shows the **Status Bar** option:

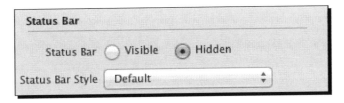

Android

As you'll see, the number of options to set for Android is less than that for iOS. This isn't so because Android is simpler, but because LiveCode exposes virtually all of the possible settings for iOS, including a lot that you will most likely not need. iOS also has the splash screen variations that are not available as options in Android.

In the Android world, there are some settings that you are required to make, in particular, the **Permissions** ones. iOS does ask the user for permission to use some features, but not until the time that your app invokes that feature. You will have seen dialog boxes that ask: **Fancy App wants to know your location**. Android on the other hand asks for permission to use those features at the time that the app is installed.

Let us look at the options for Android.

Basic Application Settings

Several of the iOS options are given a different name for Android OS. Instead of **Display Name** there is **Label**, **Internal App ID** is called **Identifier**, and there isn't a provisioning file, but there is a **Signing Key**. Essentially though, they are the same options as for iOS.

The **Icon** is set as part of the basic settings, because only one icon is needed, so no need for its own set of options. For that one icon you would select a 512x512 sized version of the image, and LiveCode will make the other sizes for you.

Android apps don't have a splash screen like that in iOS, but LiveCode can be given a splash screen, and will show that as the first screen that the user sees after the app loads.

You are able to set where the app will be installed, with choices of **Internal Storage Only**, **Allow External Storage**, and **Prefer External Storage**. The external storage being referred to is the SD memory that most Android devices can have. Android users either don't care where the app is installed, or they are fanatical about it being stored in the SD memory! You could select **Allow External Storage**, and expect a lot of people to choose to have it installed in the SD memory, or you could choose **Prefer External Storage**, knowing that only a minority would change the option to force the installation to be done into internal memory. Overall, you upset less people by using the **Prefer External Storage** setting.

In-app purchasing and push notifications, which at the time of writing are very new features in LiveCode, are handled in a different way than they are with iOS. If you wish to use in-app purchasing, take a look at the RunRev online lessons, and also the `developer.android.com` website for more information. So far there is only an iOS lesson, located here:

`http://lessons.runrev.com/m/4069/l/48771`

Presumably the Android lesson will be added to that some day soon. The Android developer information on in-app billing is here:

```
http://developer.android.com/guide/market/billing/billing_overview.
html
```

As with iOS, Android OS can be given external commands, and also has the custom URL scheme. One feature that is not to be found in iOS is the ability to set an icon to be used in the task bar.

Here is how the basic application settings options are presented:

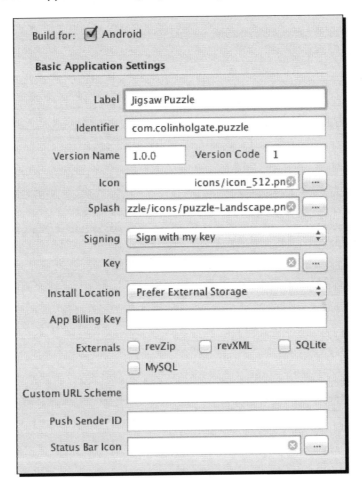

Requirements and Restrictions

Within this set of options you can set the **Minimum Android Version** and set which hardware features are required. The columns of radio buttons are named differently than iOS. Instead of saying that a feature is required or prohibited, you are saying whether the feature is required or used. This becomes information that the Android user is able to read, and may play a part in whether they choose to buy your app. So, try to select any that apply to your app.

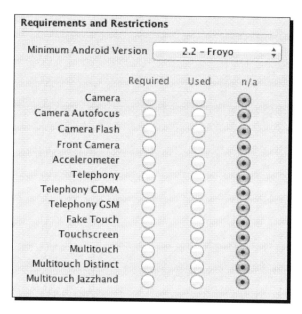

Application Permissions

When an iOS app makes use of certain features, such as your location, there is an alert dialog that appears when the feature is first used. With Android any such features are listed during the installation of the app, and the user will give permission for all the features in one go.

Here are the permissions you can choose from:

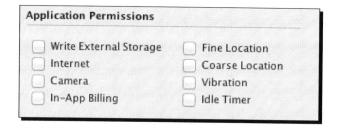

User Interface Options

The **User Interface Options** performs the same function as the orientation and status bar options in iOS. If you are submitting an iPad app that is landscape, you have to support both variations of landscape. This is not the same requirement with the Android app stores, and so the options are much simpler, you only have to say whether the **Initial Orientation** is to be **Portrait** or **Landscape**, and whether the **Status Bar** is to be **Visible** or **Hidden**:

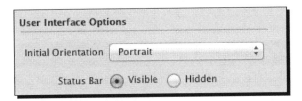

Building Apps for Beta Testers

You may have been giving test builds to friends and colleagues all the way through developing your app, but even if you haven't, it becomes more important to do so as you get closer to uploading the app to the app stores. Beta testers can tell you about technical and non-technical issues. Are there typos in the Credits? Does the icon look good? Were there any strange aspects to the installation experience? And of course, does the app do what it's supposed to do, on the numerous devices and operating systems?

The process of making an app to send to a tester is different on Android than on iOS. In fact, it's incredibly easy on Android! Let's look at that first.

Sending an Android App to testers

When you do a **Save as Standalone Application...** for Android, you create an APK file. You could e-mail that file to your testers, and they could do what is called a "side load" of the file onto their device. In Chapter 2, *Getting Started with LiveCode Mobile*, we saw how tricky it can be to get an Android device connected for testing, and it could well be beyond the technical abilities of some of your testers to do that.

Fortunately there is a much simpler approach. Take the APK file and put it online somewhere. That might be on a DropBox shared location, or Google Drive, or perhaps just a server at your office. Do whatever it takes to get to the point that you have a URL that links to the file. Now e-mail that URL to your testers, to an e-mail address that they can read on their devices. Then it only takes a single touch of the link in the email to start the downloading and installing of your app.

There is a **Development** section of the Android device settings that the testers may need to visit, to enable the feature that allows apps to be installed in this way, but it's very easy to make that change.

Preparing an iOS App so that it can work on someone else's device

Things are not quite as straightforward for iOS! The first thing you need to do is to add the **unique device ID (UDID)** for each of your beta testers' devices to your iOS developer account. Your testers can get that number by connecting the device to their computer and viewing its **Info** in iTunes. When you're looking at the **Info** tab, you will see the serial number for the device. Clicking on that number will make it change to a longer number, which is the UDID that will be needed. Once that number is showing you can do a keyboard shortcut to copy the number to the clipboard (*Command+C* on Mac, *Ctrl+C* on Windows). Have your testers do this, and then have them paste the number into an e-mail to you. You want to make sure that you get the number right, because it will use up one of your 100 devices allocation in your iOS developer account.

Go to `https://developer.apple.com/ios/manage/devices/index.action` in order to add the devices to your account. Click on the **Add Devices** button on that page, and you will be able to add the devices to your account:

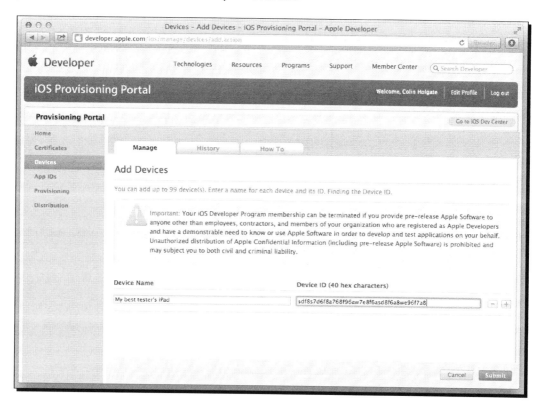

Next, go to the following link: `https://developer.apple.com/ios/manage/ provisioningprofiles/index.action` and either create a new profile, or select an existing one and choose **Edit/Modify**. You will then see a list of the devices associated with your account, and can enable any combination of devices you want to work with that provisioning profile. In the following screenshot you'll see that the pool of test devices is very short:

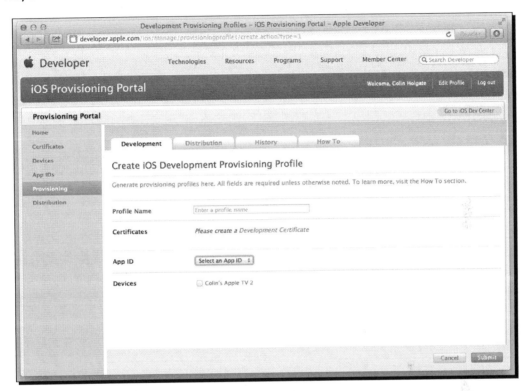

After you submit the changes you will see that the modified profile is **pending**. It doesn't take any time to process the provisioning file; you could immediately reload the page and find that it's ready to download.

Download the new profile and add it to Xcode (just double-clicking the downloaded file should do that for you). Open your app's **Mainstack** in LiveCode, go into **Standalone Application Settings... | iOS**, and make sure the provisioning profile is selected from the **Profile** menu, and **Save as Standalone Application...** again, to make sure that the new devices are known to the app.

By now you will have an APP file, which is the iOS equivalent of the APK of Android. As with Android you could e-mail that file to your testers, along with the provisioning file, and have the testers "side load" it onto their devices. In this instance that's not such a difficult task, because the tester can use iTunes to do that. If you do go that route, have your testers drag the APP file and provisioning files onto the **Library** in iTunes, connect the device, view the **Apps** tab, make sure that the new app is selected, and perform a **Sync**. However, it is possible to make things a lot easier for your users, as easy as it was for Android users.

Creating "over the air" installers for iOS

Since iOS 4.0, it has been possible to install an app from a link in a web page. Creating the file structure for that to work is a bit tricky though, but fortunately there are at least a couple of tools you can buy to make things easy for you.

AirLaunch

HyperActive Software has made a LiveCode plugin that can take your APP file and make the file structure needed for the "over the air" install to work. There is just a single dialog that you need to fill in as shown in the following:

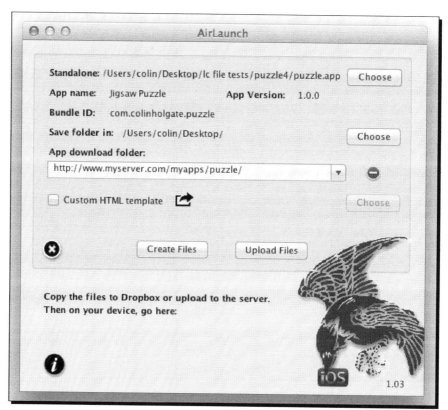

After selecting the APP file you only need to enter the URL of where the folder will be when it's online, and then click the **Create Files** button. You then e-mail the URL of that folder to your testers, and when they visit the web page on their device there will be a single link to touch, and the app will be installed.

See more information about **AirLaunch** on the page using the following link:

```
http://www.hyperactivesw.com/airlaunch/index.html
```

BetaBuilder

BetaBuilder can be found in the Mac App Store, at the following link:

```
http://itunes.apple.com/us/app/betabuilder-for-ios-apps/
id415348946?mt=12
```

It wasn't made with LiveCode in mind, and it works with IPA files, not APP files. The process is much the same as with AirLaunch; you select the file to use, enter the URL of the online folder, and the program will generate the files for you. Again, all that happens in a single dialog window as shown in the following screenshot:

An easy way to convert the LiveCode APP file into an IPA is to drag the APP into iTunes, and then select **Show in Finder** by right-clicking on the app in the **Library**. That will reveal the IPA file, which you can drag into the BetaBuilder window.

Both products make life easy for your testers. AirLaunch has the advantages of being a plugin that works within LiveCode, which you're likely to have opened anyway, and working directly with the APP files that LiveCode creates. BetaBuilder's main advantage is that it's incredibly cheap!

TestFlightApp.com

`https://testflightapp.com` uses exactly the same technique as the two applications use, but the site also includes a lot of project management tools. It's a lot more than you need for sending out personal apps to a few testers, but it may come into its own more when dealing with several apps going out to a large group of testers.

Creating an app store submission file

The biggest hurdle to overcome in order to make a version of your app that can be submitted to app stores is the acquiring of a distribution certificate. The process is quicker for Android, but does involve some typing in the command line, and there is a slight difference if you are on Windows rather than Mac. The iOS process has many steps to it, but at least those don't involve typing cryptic commands. We'll look at Android first.

Finding and using the Android Keytool application

One of the things that was installed when you added the Java Development Kit is a tool for making a **keystore** file, which is a self-assigned certificate. It's this tool that is used to create the certificate you'll need in order to distribute an Android app.

On Mac you don't need to find that application, you can simply type the command into the Terminal, and the tool is found for you. On Windows you need to navigate to the folder where Keytool lives. Before getting that far you have to first open the command line as Administrator.

On Windows, the CMD application is to be found in `C:\Windows\System32\`. Go to that directory in Windows Explorer, right-click on the file, and select **Run as Administrator**. The Keytool application will be in the bin folder of the Java JDK directory. Once you are at the C:\ prompt, change directories to get to that location, which will be something like: `C:\Program Files\Java\jdkx.x.x_xx\bin\`, where the `jdkx.x.x_xx` part would actually be the version of the JDK that you have installed. You should be able to get all the way there with a line like this:

```
C:\> cd \Program Files\Java\jdk1.7.0_01\bin\
```

On Mac you will use the Terminal, which is located in /Application/Utilites. Just open Terminal, and you'll immediately be able to use the Keytool application.

In either case you will now type a relatively short line, and then answer the various questions that appear. For a full understanding of what is going on, visit this web page:

```
http://developer.android.com/guide/publishing/app-signing.html
```

For our purposes, we'll just type in the right command and all should go well, even if we don't understand what we typed!

This is the line to type, changing the keystore and alias names to match the names you wish to use for this certificate:

```
keytool -genkey -v -keystore my-release-key.keystore
-alias alias_name -keyalg RSA -keysize 2048 -validity 10000
```

When you press the *Enter* or *Return* key you will start to see a series of questions, starting with the password you wish to use for the keystore. Further questions will ask for your full name, details about your company, city, and country. It's a set of data that can be encoded into a keystore that is unique, and has enough accurate information with which a user can decide whether to trust the certificate.

When the tool is finished you will have the keystore file that LiveCode requires. It will be easily available in your home folder on Mac, and somewhat buried in the JDK bin folder on Windows.

Go into the **Basic Application Settings** of the **Standalone Application Settings** of your **Mainstack**, and navigate to the file from the **Key** entry. Once chosen, that section will look like the following screenshot:

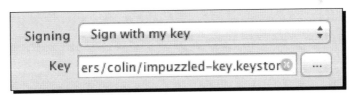

If you have chosen your icons, splash screen, requirements, and permissions, you should be able to build a version of the APK file that can be uploaded to app stores.

Creating a distribution certificate for iOS

As mentioned above, there is no command line typing involved in getting a distribution certificate for iOS, but there are a lot of steps involved. First place to visit is the iOS Developer Portal, to make sure that you have set up a dedicated **App ID** and **Provisioning** file for this particular app.

The following screenshots represent the steps taken to get a certificate and profile for an app to be named `I'm Puzzled!`, which is essentially the jigsaw puzzle that we made earlier on.

In the **App IDs** part of the portal there is a **New App ID** button that takes you to a page for entering in the App ID details. Here you can see that the ID is given the name of `Im Puzzled App ID`, and a **Bundle Identifier** of `com.colinholgate.impuzzled`. This needs to match the **Internal App ID** set in LiveCode.

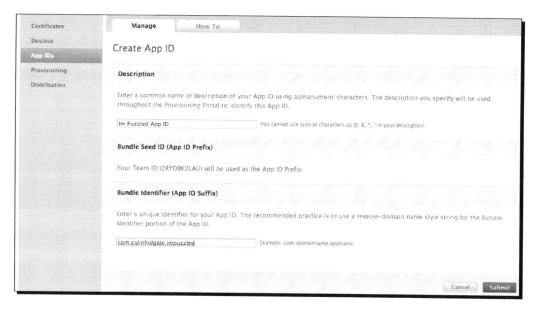

Now that there is an App ID, it can be used in setting up a **Distribution Provisioning Profile**, on the **Provisioning** section. One difficulty though is the warning message about creating a certificate:

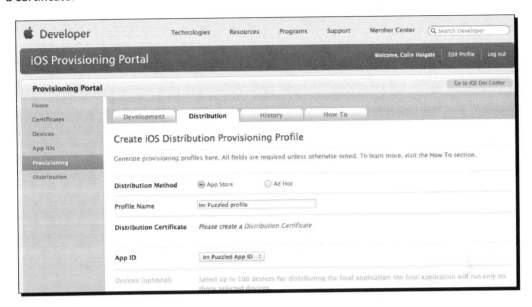

Clicking on the linked text takes you to a long description of how you have to request a certificate authority, and to upload a file that Keychain Access generates. When you encounter this situation, carefully follow the steps shown:

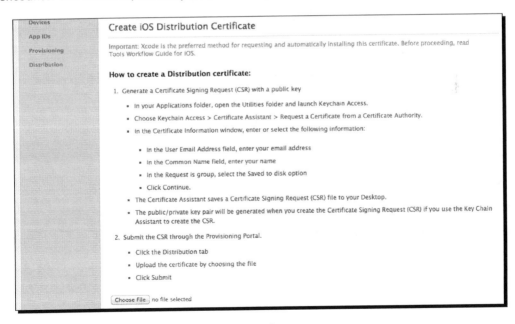

After you have uploaded that certificate request file you will be able to make a distribution profile that uses the dedicated App ID, and the distribution certificate. The final entry will look like the following screenshot, and you would use the **Download** button to get a local copy of the provisioning file:

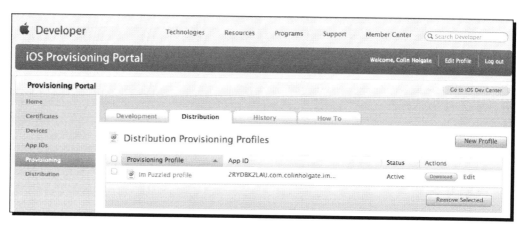

You now have the file that LiveCode requires, only you don't select it in the LiveCode settings. Instead you double-click on the file and it will install itself using Xcode. Once it is in Xcode you can then select it from the **Profile** menu in the **Basic Application Settings** in LiveCode:

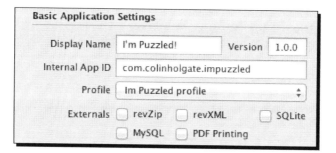

As with Android, you would make sure to add the icons and splash screens, set requirements, and so on, and you will be able to save an APP file ready to go into the iOS App Store.

Uploading to the app stores

Each app store guides you through the steps of uploading a new app, and there are quite a lot of steps involved! It could take another book to show all the screens you have to wade through. Showing those screens here would not be so valuable, mainly because of the large quantity of screens, but also because the process changes from time to time. For example, Google even changed the name of their service since Chapter 2 was written!

There is some similarity between what each of the stores will ask you, so we'll look at what preparations you might want to take before heading off to the stores. When you are ready to proceed with the upload, these are the starting pages:

- ◆ iTunes Connect - `https://itunesconnect.apple.com`
- ◆ Google Play - `https://play.google.com/apps/publish/`
- ◆ Amazon AppStore - `https://developer.amazon.com/home.html`

What's similar

All three app stores will ask for a description of what the app does, rating information, price, a support website or e-mail address, and category information. In order to ask a price, other than free, you will have to set up a merchant account. In the case of Apple, you have to give a web page address for support; Google just asks for contact information; and Amazon shows support as being optional. All three ask for screenshots, and the two Android stores also allow you to upload a demo video.

What's different

Apple asks for a lot of information that is spread over many screens. The uploading of the actual app file is handled by the **Application Loader** utility that comes as part of Xcode. It also appears that you have to enter all of the information in one sitting. Using the **Save** button at the bottom of the web page, thinking you can come back and continue later, doesn't seem to work.

Google asks for a lot of information, but it's all jammed into one screen! Be careful as you start to use the page. The first thing they ask for is the APK file. You should probably cancel that at first, because you haven't yet set a price for the app. If you do upload the APK right away, it's instantly and permanently a free app.

Amazon asks for less information, and presents the questions within one page. There are rave reviews out there, praising the ease of submitting to the Amazon AppStore!

Bottom line

The submission process is just about the most stressful part of developing a mobile app! It makes you feel better about the other stages you've been through; perhaps those weren't so bad after all!

Hopefully you have a partner who can be a second pair of eyes, to help you understand all of the questions, and not miss something vital that will haunt you later.

Summary

I don't know about you, but I'm beat! And not just because it's 4 a.m., this mobile app developing business can be overwhelming. Even the administrative side of things can be quite involved. In this chapter we covered some of those less programmatic tasks:

- Examining all of the options in the **Standalone Application Settings**
- Fighting our way through command lines and red tape to get an app certified
- Tried to get mentally prepared for submitting to app stores

We're at the end of the road as far as making use of mobile features in a LiveCode stack, and taking that through to the point of being a real mobile app. Next up, we'll look at a few add-ons to LiveCode that would enable you to use even more mobile features.

Extending LiveCode

The story so far...

The long and winding road was the last single to be released by the Beatles, and it would make a good title for a book describing what it took to get LiveCode working on mobile devices! As soon as there were apps on iPhone, RunRev was developing a way to publish to iPhone from LiveCode. Then, in April 2010, Steve Jobs wrote this infamous article on Flash:

```
http://www.apple.com/hotnews/thoughts-on-flash/
```

Adobe had also been developing a way to publish to iPhone from Flash Professional, but as part of Apple's determination to not allow anything Flash to be usable on iPhone, the App Store submission rules were changed, forbidding developers from using any tool other than Xcode to publish apps.

Some tools continued to be in a gray area, because they used Xcode to do the final publish. GameSalad and Unity apps continued to be published and did well in the App Store. RunRev tried to convince Apple to allow LiveCode (which was still called **Runtime Revolution** at the time) to be usable as a publishing tool for iPhone, even promising to only publish on iPhone, and not to pursue publishing on Android. Apple stood their ground, and declined the offer.

For Adobe, this wasn't the end of the world, and they started to work on Android publishing. But, RunRev had already planned a conference around the idea of publishing to iOS, and that conference had to be postponed.

During the summer of 2010, Apple ran a survey for developers, and several of the questions gave people like me a chance to beg Apple to allow us to use our preferred development tools, and not to have to use Xcode. It's hard to be sure if that's what made the difference, but on September 9th, 2010, Apple changed their position on the subject. Here is the post that I woke up to that morning:

```
http://www.apple.com/pr/library/2010/09/09Statement-by-Apple-on-App-
Store-Review-Guidelines.html
```

I quickly posted a message to the Revolution e-mail list, titled *how to totally make Kevin's day*, "Kevin" being Kevin Miller, CEO of RunRev. It had the desired effect, and you can still read the follow up messages:

```
http://runtime-revolution.278305.n4.nabble.com/how-to-totally-make-
Kevin-s-day-td2532866.html
```

This got RunRev back on to developing a "Publish to iOS" feature, iPhone OS having been renamed as iOS by that time. The delayed conference ended up taking place in San Jose, at the end of April 2011. By that time, RunRev had not only made the iOS feature work well, but they had also released the first version of the "Publish to Android" feature.

It's quite amusing in a way to think that if you intend to publish to Android from LiveCode, you can thank Apple for being so stubborn!

Extending LiveCode

The progress on LiveCode has continued at quite a fast pace, and by April 2012 RunRev had implemented all of the iOS features for Android too, as well as having added a lot to the feature set for iOS.

Still, not every feature is covered, and there is a third-party market of add-ons to LiveCode, which either makes developing in LiveCode easier, or that provide features that are not yet available in the standard version. Here are some of those add-ons, most of which can be bought from the LiveCode Marketplace:

```
http://www.runrev.com/store/
```

MobGUI

We have already used **MobGUI** in earlier chapters. It takes the form of a plugin. You place the MobGUI file into your `plugins` folder. This LiveCode lesson describes adding plugins:

```
http://lessons.runrev.com/s/lessons/m/4071/l/21341-how-to-install-
custom-user-plugins
```

The way that MobGUI works is that it lets you place regular LiveCode controls onto your stack's card, and then when the app is run, the standard controls are swapped for native controls. This has an advantage over just making standard controls that look like iOS controls, because the control will look correct too.

MobGUI doesn't do anything that you couldn't do with your own scripts, but it does make it a lot easier to layout and use mobile OS native controls. There is a YouTube channel for MobGUI that will show you some of the things that can be done using the tool:

```
http://www.youtube.com/user/MobGUI
```

tmControl

tmControl is a set of themes made by *Tactile Media* to let you give your LiveCode stacks a more artistic appearance. In addition to sci-fi and other themes, there is an iOS theme. Here's how it looks:

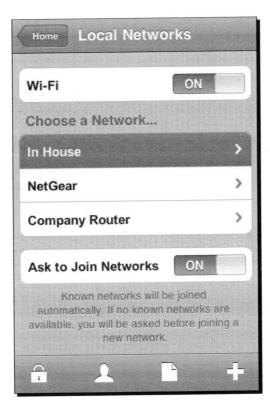

Not too surprising really! An Android theme is planned, as well as additions to the iOS theme. This page will show the currently available themes:

`http://tmtools.tactilemedia.com/tmcontrol/themes.html`

DropTools Palette

Made by Sons of Thunder Software, DropTools Palette is a free add-on to LiveCode, which acts as a shell for hosting many types of custom LiveCode controls. In addition to being the holder for Sons of Thunder custom controls, it has also been used by other developers as an easy way to bring their own custom controls to market. The DropTools website includes detailed descriptions of how you can develop your own DropTools compatible controls.

The site also acts as an "aggregator" for custom LiveCode controls, and includes links to both DropTools and non-DropTools compatible add-ons. The main page is located here:

`http://droptools.sonsothunder.com/`

Many of the custom controls do not relate to mobile apps, but there are a few, and that will no doubt increase over time.

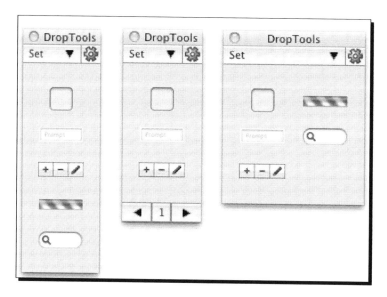

mergExt

mergExt is a suite of external commands for LiveCode. At the time of writing, there is no LiveCode Android SDK, and so currently these are all only for iOS. Here is the list as it stands, along with descriptions taken from the LiveCode Marketplace page:

http://www.runrev.com/store/product/mergExt-1-0-2/

- mergAccessory: This is an iOS external for connecting to and communicating with accessory hardware using the **External Accessory framework**.

- mergAnswerColor: This is an iOS external that presents a modal color picker.

- mergAV: This is an iOS external that adds functions and commands related to the **AVFoundation framework**. This currently includes selecting, recording, saving, and editing videos.

- mergBanner: This is an iOS external that adds an **iAd banner** to your app at the bottom of the screen.

- mergDoc: This is an iOS external that adds functions and commands related to document interaction. This currently includes presenting a modal preview, open in app menu, document options menu, and requesting the document icons in PNG form. Printing is also available via the preview.

- mergMK: This is a LiveCode MapKit external that adds a map control, which supports showing user location with heading, adding annotation pins, and polylines.

- mergMessage: This is an iOS external that adds a command to send an SMS message.

- mergPop: This is an iOS external that adds functions to present an action sheet (pop-over on iPad) and contextual menu for user interaction.

- mergReader: This is an iOS external that presents a modal PDF reader using the open source vfrReader project.

- mergSettings: This is an iOS external that integrates a LiveCode app with the **Settings** app and also includes InAppSettingsKit to present a matching dialog box from within your app.

- mergTweet: This is an iOS external that adds a command to send a tweet message.

- mergXattr: This is an iOS external that adds commands to set the do not backup and protection attributes of a file.

- mergZXing: This is a LiveCode external that uses the ZXing library to read a wide range of barcode types via the rear camera of a mobile device.

- animationEngine: This allows you to create smooth animations, and detect collisions between objects. It is well suited to both creating games and to making presentation apps. Here is its information page in the LiveCode Marketplace:

  http://runrev.com/store/product/animation-engine-5/

Although not specifically for mobile use, `animationEngine` has been adjusted to comply with iOS App Store requirements, and so should still be of use in making iOS apps. It also works for Android apps.

As shown in *Creating over the air installers for iOS* in the last chapter, AirLaunch is an add-on that makes it easy to create over-the-air installer files for iOS. A detailed description can be found here: `http://www.hyperactivesw.com/airlaunch/index.html`

Creating your own add-ons

The two main types of add-ons that you might be interested in making are custom controls and external commands and functions (generally referred to as **externals**).

Custom controls

Custom controls are typically made of a group that holds many standard controls, and with a group script that manages the appearance and interactions of those controls. There is a tutorial on making such a custom control at this page:

```
http://www.runrev.com/developers/lessons-and-tutorials/tutorials/
advanced-custom-controls/
```

If you intend to go on to make a nice custom palette to make it easy to drag-and-drop your custom controls onto the card window, consider making it DropTools-compatible. You would save yourself a significant amount of time solving the issue that DropTools already solves, and your custom controls would fit in with the other DropTools controls, making the screen less crowded with custom palettes! There is a lot of information on developing DropTools compatible controls at this page:

```
http://droptools.sonsothunder.com/developer/
```

Externals

Down the right side of the previously-mentioned "lessons-and-tutorials" page is a long list of tutorials, two of which relate to making externals. Those particular tutorials are intended for developing externals for desktop applications. For developing mobile externals, you should look at this page:

```
http://www.runrev.com/developers/documentation/externals-sdk/
```

At the time of writing, this page only covers iOS externals, but there is reason to hope that by the time you are reading this, there will be information on creating Android externals too. The page is quite a long one, and even includes a 17-minute video! The video can be viewed on YouTube too, at this address:

```
http://www.youtube.com/watch?feature=player_embedded&v=lqduyQkhigg
```

Creating externals is not trivial. If you have an idea for a useful external, but feel it's beyond your abilities or interest to create yourself, take a look at the mergExt site:

```
http://mergext.com
```

Here you can make suggestions or vote for externals that you would like to see created.

If you do feel you can make externals, why not make them available as products? The going rate for these add-ons is in the $30-$100 range - any sales you make will offset your development costs.

Pop Quiz Answers

Chapter 1, LiveCode Fundamentals

Pop Quiz – best name?

Answer: Henry. In the early days of multimedia it seemed like everyone had one of just a few names. There was Bill Atkinson, who created HyperCard, and Bill Appleton, who created SuperCard. Kevin Calhoun was the lead HyperCard programmer for a while, and Kevin Miller is the head of RunRev. Bob Stein was one of the founders of The Voyager Company, and along with Bob Abel was one of the pioneers in multimedia. Dan was another good choice, with there being Dan Winkler, author of the HyperTalk language, and Danny Goodman, author of many famous programming books. Henry would be a good name if you wanted to make motorcars, or marry lots of queens.

Pop quiz – try to remember...

Answer: The Text Formatting section of the Inspector palette. Getting to that section involved selecting the **Edit** tool, clicking on the title field, and choosing **Text Formatting** from the **Inspector** palette drop-down menu. However, there is indeed a **Text** menu. Really that's what we should have used!

Chapter 2, Getting Started with LiveCode Mobile

Pop quiz – when is something too much?

Answer: The file size is going to go over 50 MB. The other answers are valid too, though you could play the music as an external sound, to reduce loading time, but by going over 50 MB you would then cut out potential sales from people who are connected by cellular and not wireless networks. At the time of writing, all of the stores require that you be connected via wireless if you intend to download apps that are over 50 MB.

Pop quiz – tasty code names

Answer: Lemon Cheesecake. The pattern, if it isn't obvious, is that the code name takes on the next letter of the alphabet, is a kind of food, but more specifically it's a dessert food. "Munchies" almost works, but "Marshmallow" or "Meringue Pie" would be better choices!

Pop quiz – iOS code names

Answer: Hunter Mountain. Although not publicized, Apple does use code names for each version of iOS. Previous examples have included Big Bear, Apex, Kirkwood, and Telluride. These, and all of the others apparently, are ski resorts. Hunter Mountain is a relatively small mountain (3,200 feet), so if it does get used perhaps it would be a minor update!

Chapter 3, Building User Interfaces

Pop quiz – getting the big picture

Answer: 45 The original Mac had a screen that was 512x342 pixels. That will fit more than 45 times into the area of an 8-megapixel photo.

Pop quiz – the cost of things these days

Answer: 6,000 times better. Yes indeed. 25 years ago Apple was selling a 4 MB add-on kit for the Macintosh II, for about $1500. They now sell an 8 GB add-on for the Mac Pro for $500.

Chapter 4, Using Remote Data and Media

Pop quiz – name that structure

Answer: The Message Path. For further reading, RunRev has an online lesson that describes the message path:

```
http://lessons.runrev.com/s/lessons/m/4603/l/44036-the-livecode-
message-path
```

Pop quiz – other special places

Answer: Users. `Home` and `Desktop` are not used by Android, and `Desktop` is not used by iOS. `0x000e` sounded suspicious, but is actually the `specialFolderPath` entry for `My Videos`, under Unix! None of the systems has a `Users` entry.

Chapter 5, Making a Jigsaw Puzzle Application

Pop-Quiz – how many bits in a byte?

Answer: 8. If only for the interest of mathematicians, it's good to know that a byte is 8 bits. A "bit" is a "binary digit", and when you start to think of bits in those terms you will see that a byte can store 2 to the power of 8 values in it ("binary" being Base 2). That came into play when looking at the length of a Pascal string (2 to the power of 8 is 256, hence the range of characters in a Pascal String is 0-255), and it helps you realize that if a picture is made up of one byte for each pixel's red, green, and blue values, it's a 24-bit picture. Once you add in another byte of data for the alpha channel, you have a 32 bit picture.

Pop-Quiz – getting the big picture

Answer: Depends on the nature of the image. SVG is a description of how to draw the image, whereas PNG is a description of the pixels in the image. In PNG that information is also data compressed, in a lossless way. For the example map, at its original size, a 24-bit PNG is half the size of the SVG file. There is a lot of data needed to describe the outlines of the US states! If the image needs to be enlarged, the PNG file would become bigger, while the SVG would remain the same file size. On the other hand, if an image was a rectangle of a diagonal gradient the SVG would be tiny, and the PNG would be huge, because there are no long runs of same colored pixels for the data compression to work well.

Pop-Quiz – calculate this!

Answer: 16,777,216 buttons. As with the discussion about "bits and bytes", red, green, and blue values combine to give us 2 to the power of 24 possible values. If you only used two of the colors, then the answer would have been 65,536.

Chapter 6, Making a Reminders Application

Pop-Quiz – AO (Odd Acronyms!)

Answer: So as not to upset the French, sort of. The French may not have proactively objected, but indeed, the acronym of UTC was chosen so as to not specifically match the English version of the phrase. It also fell in nicely with the other acronyms of UT0, UT1, and so on.

Pop-Quiz – What floor is my apartment on?

Answer: 11th floor. The numbers coming back from the location sensor return as latitude, longitude, and elevation. That would make the elevation for where the device was at that time about 37.5 meters, much too low to be the 40th floor. There is enough information in the screenshot for you to know exactly when it was taken, and where on Earth!

Index

getdistance function 179
getPixel function 132
  about 133
  testing 134, 136
Gimp 133
GMT 161
Google Play
  URL 209
GPS 164
Graphical User Interface (GUI) 170
Greenwich Mean Time. *See* GMT

H

handlers 14
heirarchy, LiveCode
  cards, creating 15
  code 14
  stack structure 14
home card scripts
  about 177
  adding, to reminders app 178-180
HyperActive Software 202
HyperCard 8

I

Icons area, iOS section 192
image
  selecting, for jigsaw puzzle 146-151
imageData
  about 133
  misusing 134
  transferring 151-154
image data format 132, 133
ImageDataTest stack 139
inspector palette
  about 11
  used, in simple calculator application 18
installers
  creating, for iOS 202
interface controls
  about 28
  rollover buttons 28-30
  still image control 28
  Video player control 28
iOS
  distribution certificate, creating for 206-208

installers, creating for 202
  testing 64
  testing, iOS simulator used 64
iOS App
  preparing 200, 202
iOS code names 57
iOS developer
  becoming 49-56
iOS SDKs
  LiveCode, pointing to 59, 60
iOS section
  about 189
  Basic Application Settings 191, 192
  Build for settings 190
  Custom URL Scheme 194
  Icons area 192
  Orientation Options 194
  Requirements and Restrictions options 194
  Splash Screens 193
  Status Bar option 195
iOS simulator
  using 64
iTunes Connect
  URL 209

J

jigsaw puzzle
  creating 146
  imageData, transferring 151-154
  image, selecting 146-151
  pieces, creating 146-151
  touch events, setting up 155-157

K

Keepers card
  about 125
  setting up 126-128
keystore file 204
Kindle Fire
  adding, to ADB 62, 63
  using 61

L

layouts, using LiveCode Geometry Manager
  about 93

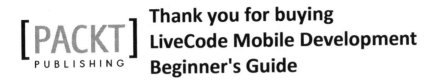

Thank you for buying
LiveCode Mobile Development
Beginner's Guide

About Packt Publishing

Packt, pronounced 'packed', published its first book "Mastering phpMyAdmin for Effective MySQL Management" in April 2004 and subsequently continued to specialize in publishing highly focused books on specific technologies and solutions.

Our books and publications share the experiences of your fellow IT professionals in adapting and customizing today's systems, applications, and frameworks. Our solution-based books give you the knowledge and power to customize the software and technologies you're using to get the job done. Packt books are more specific and less general than the IT books you have seen in the past. Our unique business model allows us to bring you more focused information, giving you more of what you need to know, and less of what you don't.

Packt is a modern, yet unique publishing company, which focuses on producing quality, cutting-edge books for communities of developers, administrators, and newbies alike. For more information, please visit our website: www.PacktPub.com.

Writing for Packt

We welcome all inquiries from people who are interested in authoring. Book proposals should be sent to author@packtpub.com. If your book idea is still at an early stage and you would like to discuss it first before writing a formal book proposal, contact us; one of our commissioning editors will get in touch with you.

We're not just looking for published authors; if you have strong technical skills but no writing experience, our experienced editors can help you develop a writing career, or simply get some additional reward for your expertise.

PUBLISHING

Sencha Touch Cookbook

ISBN: 978-1-849515-44-3   Paperback:350 pages

Over 100 recipes for creating HTML-5-based
cross-platform apps for touch devices

1. Master cross platform application development

2. Incorporate geo location into your apps

3. Develop native looking web apps

PhoneGap Mobile Application
Development Cookbook

ISBN: 978-1-849518-58-1   Paperback: 316 pages

Over 50 recipes to create mobile applications using the
PhoneGap API with examples and clear instructions

1. Use the PhoneGap API to create native mobile
   applications that work on a wide range of mobile
   devices

2. Discover the native device features and functions
   you can access and include within your applications

3. Packed with clear and concise examples to show
   you how to easily build native mobile applications

Please check **www.PacktPub.com** for information on our titles

Cocos2d for iPhone 1 Game Development Cookbook

ISBN: 978-1-849514-00-2   Paperback:446 pages

Over 90 recipes for iOS 2D game development using cocos2d

1. Discover advanced Cocos2d, OpenGL ES, and iOS techniques spanning all areas of the game development process

2. Learn how to create top-down isometric games, side-scrolling platformers, and games with realistic lighting

3. Full of fun and engaging recipes with modular libraries that can be plugged into your project

Corona SDK Mobile Game Development: Beginner's Guide

ISBN: 978-1-849691-88-8   Paperback: 408 pages

Create monetized games for iOS and Android with minimum cost and code

1. Build once and deploy your games to both iOS and Android

2. Create commercially successful games by applying several monetization techniques and tools

3. Create three fun games and integrate them with social networks such as Twitter and Facebook

Please check **www.PacktPub.com** for information on our titles

Printed in Great Britain
by Amazon.co.uk, Ltd.,
Marston Gate.